WITHDRAWN

Nicholas Rubakin
A Life for Books

N. A. and L. A. Rubakin

Nicholas Rubakin
A Life for Books

ALFRED ERICH
SENN

ÖΠP

Newtonville, Mass.
1977

ISBN 0-89250-125-1 (cloth)
    0-89259-126-X (paper)

For a brochure outlining our Russian
Biography Series, write to Dr. P.H.
Clendenning, Editor, Biography Series,
Oriental Research Partners, Box 158,
Newtonville, Mass. 02160.

Production in association with Book Production Consultants
Cambridge, England

Printed in Great Britain

CONTENTS

I INTRODUCTION: EARLY YEARS AND TRAINING

Nicholas A. Rubakin, the noted bibliographer and popular writer, was born on July 1, 1862, in Oranienbaum, Russia, and he died on November 23, 1946, in Lausanne, Switzerland. His father, Alexander Yosifovich Rubakin, came from a long line of Old Believer merchants, who had originated in Pskov. His mother, Lidya Terentievna, nee Tikhonov, also came from a merchant family of Old Believers. Alexander Yosifovich wanted both his sons, Nicholas and Michael, to become merchants, but Lidya Terentievna insisted on their higher education. Michael eventually became a factory inspector and, much in contrast to Nicholas, a *bon vivant*. Nicholas, on the other hand, inherited his mother's love of books, and he chose to make books his life.

Nicholas Rubakin liked to refer to himself as a *skromnyi knizhnyi cherviak*, a humble book worm, but he came further into the world than such a modest sobriquet would indicate. For him, books and people were inseparable. His bookplate read, "Long live the book, a powerful weapon in the struggle for truth and justice." He revered books, and he collected them assiduously. He hated to part with any of them; as his son explained, "For him books were the capital of human reason, of human knowledge. . . He loved books not for their exteriors but for their contents."[1]

For Rubakin, books represented people, the people who wrote them and the people who read them. A library served as the intermediary between author and reader, and so Rubakin dedicated his life to library work. An avid reader himself, he further contributed to the book process by offering advice to readers and by publishing recommendatory bibliographies. He also wrote prolificly: short stories, popular science, and cultural studies.

By Rubakin's own count, made in 1934, he published over 280 books and brochures: 233 of them for "readers from the toiling masses" and 49 for intellectuals. These included 15 guides for self-education. Tsarist censorship banned 47 and 3 were destroyed abroad. From 1889 to 1923, his works appeared in 20,000,000 copies in 24 languages. The Soviet government republished 22 of his works in a total of 1,400,000 copies between 1919 and 1923, and from 1923 to 1929 it put out 23 of his works in a total of 166,000 copies.[2]

Above all, Rubakin's passion was the education which books could bring to the people of Russia. A graduate of St. Petersburg University, he encouraged education in any form, whether at universities or through self-education, *samoobrazovanie*. To be sure, he had little interest in the primary education of children; he concentrated his efforts on the individual, however illiterate, who had already demonstrated an interest in reading. His son declared that only at the age of ten or eleven did he begin to receive his father's attention in such matters.[3] Rubakin concerned himself with the substance of ideas and concepts, not with basic techniques of learning. For him reading was the road to education; once a person knew how to read, all the knowledge of mankind was available to him.

In the course of his career with books, Rubakin came into contact with a wide variety of people, and his friends represented the whole Russian political spectrum at the turn of the twentieth century. He worked with Leo Tolstoy; as a member of the Socialist Revolutionary Party he had dealings with Evno Azef; his work in the education of workers brought him into contact with Nadezhda Krupskaia; he lent books to George Plekhanov and Anatole Lunacharsky; and he considered Paul Miliukov a friend. Rubakin's work both reflected and contributed to the intellectual character of the revolutionary movement in Tsarist Russia.[4]

Rubakin has fared rather poorly at the hands of historians. Even though the Soviet government granted him a pension in 1930, the culture of Stalin's Russia had no place for him. When he died in Switzerland in 1946, the Lenin Library in Moscow obtained his books and most of his papers, but his name still remained virtually unknown until the late 1950s. In recent years, interest in his career has grown significantly, but even today in the Soviet Union his bibliographical work is far better known than his intellectual and political endeavors.[5] Western writers who have taken note of him, on the other hand, have tended to offer only superficial, one-sided views of his political efforts.[6]

This study proposes to examine not so much Rubakin's own personal and intellectual development as his place in the history of the Russian revolutionary movement and in Russian cultural and intellectual life. Especially in the decade before the revolutions of 1917 Rubakin's library in Baugy-sur-Clarens served as a major center for revolutionary intellectuals and influenced their choice of reading materials.

****

Throughout his life Rubakin repeatedly expressed his intellectual indebtedness to his mother. He dedicated his most important work, *Sredi knig* (Among Books), to her memory, as having "worked twenty years among books and taught me to love the book and to believe in its insuperable and clear strength."[7] Rubakin's son, Alexander Niko-laevich, said of his grandmother, "She first directed his mind and will in the direction of writing; she first aroused his passion for science and for books. But this passion did not remain just a passion demanding satisfaction, but rather the very basis of his life. Thanks to his mother, my father did not become a merchant or a bureaucrat; he did not sink into the morass of unenlightened philistinism."[8]

Lidya Terentievna was very much the enlightened woman of the 1860s in Russia. She read progressive literature, rolled her own ciga-rettes, smoked in public, and at one time attended a revolutionary circle which was frequented by the well known radical writer D. I. Pisarev. She had largely educated herself, since her father had opposed her schooling.

When it came time for her two sons to enter gymnasium, Lidya Terentievna resolved her husband's doubts about sending the boys to St. Petersburg by moving the entire family to the capital in 1873. In 1875, at Nicholas' urging, she opened a private library, buying books for 60 rubles and taking many more on credit. In all she obtained about 600 books, and the collection, which in 1892 numbered 7,000 volumes, soon became the largest private library in the city.

In his first years in St. Petersburg, Nicholas displayed a rather nonchalant attitude toward his formal schooling. He disliked his teachers, and he often failed to attend classes. By himself, however, he studied enthusiastically, working with his mother in the library. In 1877 he sold his first article, receiving sixteen rubles for a study, "The Deification of Animals," which he published in a journal on children's literature.[9] By 1879 he was regularly placing articles in popular journals, and he had compiled two catalogs of the holdings of his mother's library.[10]

In the late 1870s, Rubakin began to read revolutionary literature, and in 1880 he became acquainted with the writings of Auguste Comte. It was under the influence of Comte's principles of encyclopedic educa-tion that Rubakin chose to study in all three faculties when he entered the University of St. Petersburg in the fall of 1880. He was enrolled formally in the physical-mathematical faculty, since this taught the "exact sciences" but he diligently attended lectures and courses in both of the other faculties, law and historical-philological.[11]

The decade of the 1880s, in which Rubakin came to maturity, was one of governmental reaction. Tsar Alexander II had been killed by a terrorist bomb in March of 1881, and under his son, Alexander III,

Russia endured a much more oppressive regime. After their enthusiastic campaigns of the 1870s of attempting "to go to the people", many intellectuals now concentrated on "small deeds," cultural work.[12] This course was especially appealing to Rubakin, who participated in socialist study groups and distributed literature. For his efforts, he was arrested in October 1884 and was put under police surveillance for one year. This arrest apparently cost Rubakin his chance for a university teaching career.[13]

Rubakin occasionally insisted that he had become a revolutionary in this period under the influence of the execution of Alexander Ulianov, the older brother of Vladimir Ilich Lenin. Rubakin had known Ulianov, had participated in a study circle with him, and had written a melancholy poem after his execution. On the other hand, Rubakin frequently romanticized his past in accordance with his evaluation of his audience and his references to Ulianov were strongest in the petitions which he submitted to the Soviet government during the 1920s in his efforts to receive a pension or some other kind of official support. While disturbed by Ulianov's execution, Rubakin probably did not veer far from his fundamental belief in education as the fundamental vehicle for the liberation of the toiling masses.

Rubakin was also influenced by other contemporaries. In later reflecting on those whom he considered "the great figures of the Russian Revolution,"[14] Rubakin chose to include two women from the era of his student days: Catherine Breshko-Breshkovskaia and Vera Figner. He considered them entirely different types of revolutionary personalities. Breshkovskaia was above all a "person of the heart, an emotional type," while Figner, the "most remarkable" of the Russian terrorists and the "Russian Charlotte Corday," was a person of "mind and will, a strong willed type."

Rubakin particularly admired Breshkovskaia, the "grandmother of the revolution," who had left her husband in the early 1870s to participate in the movement "to the people," aimed at arousing the revolutionary consciousness of the Russian peasantry. Rubakin considered the "babushka" better able than most members of the intelligentsia to communicate with the peasantry, and he viewed her as virtually a religious figure: "All her cult of revolution was founded on service to man and on her great love for him. That was above all a cult of the revolutionary heart."

Vera Figner attracted him not as a terrorist but as a martyr. He was a student in St. Petersburg when she was sentenced to twenty years' imprisonment for her part in the assassination of Tsar Alexander II. The students of the 1880s passed around pictures of Vera Figner in prison and sympathized with her martyrdom. In Rubakin's case this image was later emphasized, after her release from prison, by her retirement to Switzerland, where Rubakin saw her almost daily in the last years before the First World War. She visited his home for musical evenings and went for walks with his children. Most of all, Rubakin sympathized with her lost years in prison.

By the time he wrote these descriptions, in the early 1920s, Rubakin was much more under the influence of Tolstoyan teachings than he had been in the 1880s, but nevertheless he had always tended to favor revolution through education rather than through violence. In writing of Figner, he declared, "Every act of violence calls forth still greater violence." Terrorists, he noted, "always blame not themselves but their opponents for the terrorism, and they do not note their own terrorism or else they justify it: 'It is less than our opponents'."[15]

In the long run, Rubakin was probably most influenced during the 1880s by the establishment of Posrednik, a publishing house staffed by followers of Tolstoy, which in 1885 began to publish cheap editions of the master's works for mass distribution. Inexpensive books were of themselves not a new phenomenon, but inexpensive editions of the works of great authors had been a rarity; as Rubakin put it, "Up to that time no great writer had penetrated to the popular masses." Other publishing houses subsequently followed this lead, but Rubakin insisted on crediting Tolstoy and his followers with having led the way.[16] Posrednik, he insisted, "marked a turning point in Russian popular literature."[17]

Rubakin worked with Posrednik and later insisted that he had learned the "art of propaganda" from Tolstoy. In Russia, Rubakin explained, most peasants were illiterate, and their vocabulary comprised perhaps 10,000 words, while intellectuals might command 75,000 words. "The intellectuals and the people," he declared, "literally spoke two different languages." Under these circumstances, raising the cultural level of the mass of the population posed enormous problems, and Rubakin, who devoted his life to this task, felt that he had learned the most from Tolstoy.

Tolstoy argued that the intelligentsia had to understand the ways of the masses: "What right has privileged liberal society to educate the alien people according to its own pattern? This cannot be explained by anything other than a crude egoistic delusion." At the same time, Tolstoy insisted that the masses had to receive an education which was morally uplifting: "Without ethics, even simple literacy is dangerous."[18]

Tolstoy and Rubakin were not without their differences. In 1892, the novelist criticized Rubakin's educational works. "Why do you write mostly books on science for the people?" Tolstoy questioned. "The people do not need this. They need the science of life: 'How to live,' 'Where is its meaning?'" Rubakin disagreed, insisting that "exact knowledge is the best means of struggling with dark superstitious orthodoxy." Tolstoy nevertheless persisted, arguing, "No, write instead about drunkenness, against smoking tobacco."[19]

As a young man in his early twenties, Rubakin, to be sure, did not immediately respond to Tolstoy's teachings. Only with time did Tolstoy's influence on him grow, largely as the result of Rubakin's association in the emigration several decades later with P. I. Biriukov and also through his second wife. In the late 1880s, Rubakin was still seeking his way through the kaleidoscope of political and cultural influences which he met in St. Petersburg.

When Rubakin completed his university work in 1887, his parents urged him to enter government service.[20] Rubakin refused, but after his marriage in 1888 to Nadezhda Ivanovna Ignatiev, who soon bore him a son, Alexander, he agreed to join his brother and his father in operating a paper mill. The father handled the business affairs, Michael looked after technical matters, and Nicholas took it upon himself to handle the books and to deal with the workers. In 1891 the business failed, but Rubakin now had had direct experience in dealing with workers. He chose to leave the business life and to dedicate himself to literary activity.[21]

He had already begun investigating the relationship of books and readers. In 1888 he had organized a group, associated with Posrednik, to study popular literature. Noting how differently readers might react to a given book, he began to develop programs for self-education. In 1889 he published his first program for individual study.[22] He further developed his ideas by corresponding with readers, advising them as he perceived their wants and needs. Between 1889 and his departure from Russia in 1907, Rubakin wrote to 5189 readers.[23] He also made annual trips through European Russia and the Caucasus, visiting factories and villages and studying "the psychology of the laboring classes, their economic situation and way of life."[24]

By the early 1890s Rubakin had also embarked on a program of writing popular works on scientific subjects. His first two efforts, on nature (1892) and on the animal kingdom (1893), quickly became classics, and he soon acquired a great reputation as a popular writer of this genre.[25]

Rubakin argued strongly at this time that the workers could develop their own intelligentsia. In his later writings, he insisted that this was then a novel and revolutionary idea, since most intellectuals thought that the intelligentsia had to come from disaffected elements of the middle and upper classes.[26] He often liked to recall that in 1890 after a speech on this topic, he received a congratulatory visit from two women who strongly agreed with him, the wife of the historian M. I. Tugan-Baranovsky and Nadezhda Konstantinovna Krupskaia, later to be the wife of V. I. Lenin. He and Krupskaia subsequently became close friends, and he considered her as one of the "truly remarkable, stubborn workingwomen, very adroitly able to serve two gods at once: both culture and revolution."[27]

In 1892 Rubakin took over the operation of his mother's library in St. Petersburg. Lidya Terentievna's collection had become an important part of the cultural scene in St. Petersburg. It served both intelligentsia and workers' education groups. Soviet writers have called it one of the first legal institutions to provide Marxist circles with free literature.[28] Nevertheless the library had had financial difficulties in recent years, and Lidya Terentievna was faced with the prospect of having to sell it.

Rubakin completely reorganized the collection, and he now formally and irreversibly launched his own library and literary career. He was already well known in St. Petersburg for his educational activities, but it was as a librarian and bibliographer that he was to become the intimate of many leading figures of the Russian revolutionary movement. As Rubakin became well known, the intellectuals actively sought him out. Upon meeting Rubakin, the narodnik Nicholas K. Mikhailovsky reportedly declared, "Reubakin, I don't know you, but I love you very much."[29]

II THE PETERSBURG YEARS

From 1892 to 1907 Rubakin lived mainly in St. Petersburg, directing his mother's library, which he inherited upon her death in 1905. He expanded its holdings from some 7000 volumes to 115,000 and greatly broadened its activities, offering a variety of services to subscribers and developing cooperative ventures with other institutions.[1] In 1907, on the eve of his departure from Russia, Rubakin donated the collection to the All-Russian League for Education, keeping for himself a basic collection of just 7000 volumes. Unfortunately the league was not up to the task of caring for the books, and in the following years the library was dissolved and the books were scattered.[2]

On the occasion of the donation of his collection, Rubakin gave a speech entitled "Basic Tasks of Library Work," in which he expounded his philosophy at some length.[3] Library work, Rubakin asserted, was not just a matter of *biukhervurmstvo;* it entailed serious social responsibilities. The library must have a democratic structure, providing books to those people who really needed them, who were the most deprived of wealth under the capitalist system. The library must be responsive to social psychology and to the given historical moment. The library represents "a weapon of society in the struggle for a better future." It should be "a sort of nursery for the most useful social microbes. Each book should be such a microbe; these microbes should fly in all directions from our organism, with our, gentlemen, specifically our planned and conscious help."

Rubakin believed that there should be no limitation on the size of a library, and that it should welcome any contribution of books. At the same time, the collection should have a "nucleus," which would enable it to serve as an encyclopedia of knowledge of all the sciences. For this purpose, of course, it had to be well cataloged, and Rubakin recommended Comte's classification of human knowledge as a workable key to the universe.

The catalog, moreover, should help all readers, even the least prepared. Books should be ranked according to their degree of difficulty so that the reader could have the "practical possibility to progress forward and upward in any science." In turn, the libraries must respond to the "given historical moment" by organizing sections on "the history of Russian social movements," on "the history of students," and on "agricultural and urban self-government." Rubakin also made a strong plea for the collection of newspapers, which become "bibliographical rarities" on the day after their publication. He paid special attention to the necessity of reference and bibliographical sections in the library.

Rubakin added some intriguing recommendations for librarians on how to collect books, declaring that he himself had used these tactics successfully. Besides the usual channels of purchase or wheedling free copies from publishers, Rubakin urged the public librarians to compete with bookdealers to make certain that private libraries were given as a whole to social institutions rather than broken up for the used book trade. Another source of books lay in competing with the bookdealers in obtaining duplicates being discarded by the Imperial Public Library.

When it came to problems of getting the books into circulation—"the book does not do its job standing on the shelf"—Rubakin spoke of the necessity of studying the "coefficient of refraction" of the given reader. "Different readers react differently to the same book, and vice versa, different books react similarly on one reader, depending on the latter's psyche, which is itself a function of many variables." Rubakin eventually codified these thoughts as his theory of "bibliopsychology," but in 1907 he spoke of this field of study as "aesthetopsychology."

Matching the book with the reader was a complicated task, but it was an enormously important one: "If the task of studying the reading public in every country were taken up on psychological and sociological foundations, this would make it possible for science to explain the contemporary historical moment as no historian could, and no economist." For the moment, however, this was obviously impossible, and it remained for every public library to study its own constituency, either individually or en masse.

In 1900, on the occasion of his library's 25th anniversary, Rubakin had already made clear his view of the areas in which a library should concentrate: "In the properly organized library the scientific section ought to occupy the first place. In second place should be the literary, belletristic section." By *belles lettres*, Rubakin understood not just novelists and poets, but also moralists, publicists, and critics: "The belletristic section is a reflection of the history of human strivings."[4]

Rubakin's work drew its share of criticism. Some bibliographers scorned his theoretical principles, and one, K. M. Derunov, focused on Rubakin's refusal to weed his collection. Derunov firmly believed in the necessity of discarding books of low quality. Rubakin did not want to discard anything; a reader who sought trash should be weaned to better things, not just ignored. Derunov's position on this question, it should be noted, has drawn sympathetic treatment by Soviet bibliographers, even though Derunov's own recommendatory bibliography listed far fewer revolutionary authors than did Rubakin in his works.[5]

Rubakin's library work demanded a great deal of his time, but he made little profit from it. In 1903, for example, Rubakin's records showed income of 8500 rubles and expenditures of 8440 rubles, leaving a net income of just 60 rubles.[6] He had to rely on his writing to provide himself with the basic necessities of life.

From 1894 to 1897 Rubakin served as director of the publishing house of O. N. Popov. For the next two years, he headed a special division for scientific and popular-scientific books in Ivan D. Sytin's publishing house, but he had to leave that position because of troubles with the censorship.[7] In 1901 Rubakin directed the house of Alekseev, and at various times he held stock in several other firms.

In his writing, Rubakin considered himself a publicist. His topics included popular scientific works, bibliographical works and studies of the reading public, a few efforts at fiction, and political tracts composed for both the Socialist Revolutionary Party, with which he associated himself, and also the Social Democrats. His studies of the Russian bureaucracy became classics which revolutionaries diligently read and frequently cited.[8] In the estimate of one Soviet commentator, he used "official statistical material and on this basis drew sharp political conclusions directed against the government, the higher bureaucracy, the nobility, and the clergy. In popular, often satirical form, N. A. Rubakin explained complicated questions of politics, topical questions of social life and governmental activity which concerned everyone, and he thereby joined the broad masses of readers to political life, preparing the soil for active participation in the class struggle."[9]

Rubakin himself explained the popularity of his writings as having developed from a number of factors: their vital character arising from their direct connection with the daily lives of the readers; their psychological outlook; their clear style; their emotional tone; their revolutionizing strength; their topicality and concrete exposition; the author's revolutionary attitude toward all the general slogans of the day; his sharply negative attitude toward the church and the government; and the allusions which formed a bond between the author and others opposed to the government.[10]

In such work, Rubakin devoted a great deal of effort to defining the role and character of the Russian intelligentsia. Writing in 1922, he insisted that one must not confuse the term "intelligentsia" with the "group of educated people." Education alone was not enough to make a person an intellectual (*intelligent*), and a person who had not even been to school could be considered an intellectual under certain circumstances. In Russia, the intelligentsia was the "social group which expresses within itself 'the mind, the feelings, and the conscience of the people and its idealistic strivings for light, for truth, for justice, for good, and for general happiness.'"[11]

At the beginning of the 20th century, Rubakin pictured the intelligentsia as consisting of two parts: those belonging to the "pure public," *chistaia publika*, who were satisfied to live within the existing political and social order, and those who put their intelligence and education at the service of the people. These latter had joined with intellectuals arising from the ranks of the working people to struggle with the burning issues of the day: "An intellectual not taking part in the struggle for the resolution of the basic tasks of his time is in essence not an intellectual at all, since he lacks the basic mark of an intellectual, his capacity for struggle."[12]

Rubakin considered it difficult for the intellectual to maintain his dedication to revolutionary principles and to avoid slipping into the ranks of the "pure public." He vividly described this problem in an essay entitled "The Demagnetized Intellectual" (*Razmagnichennyi intelligent*), which was republished several times. Having narrowed and reduced his goals, a friend of Rubakin's had lost the spirit of his student days and had sunk into concerns about living "his own private life." A man, Rubakin wrote, naturally seeks to imagine himself a hero and a struggler, but in concentrating on details of his daily life, he deceives himself, loses his purpose in life, and eventually "demagnetizes" his drive to better society.[13] Maxim Gorky called this essay a "remarkably neat characterization of the spiritual death of an intellectual."[14]

In a short story entitled "Professor Sturmwelt's Bomb," he depicted another such intellectual of the "pure public," a German from Westphalia, who had invented the ultimate weapon, a bomb containing a bacillus called "microspirula Sturmweltii." Developed as a serum against cholera, the bacillus could be used to kill or simply to incapacitate an enemy. Prof. Sturmwelt offered this weapon to his government, and the cabinet minister, to whom he spoke and who bore no name, quickly overcame his first feelings of revulsion and agreed to bring the offer to the "sovereign." Prof. Sturmwelt, who described the symptoms caused by the bacillus with great enthusiasm, had acted from motives of personal gain, and the minister had thought only of power in a Europe "inhabited not by people with flesh and nerves but by some abstract creatures, red, black, blue, white, not thinking or feeling, which could be assembled and dispersed, armed and disarmed."[15]

In contrast to such intellectuals, Rubakin called for dedication and self-sacrifice on behalf of the people. The masses, and especially the factory workers, he argued, had a great desire to read and to learn. From their ranks would come a "new force, a force of thinking destroyers and thinking, self-conscious creators—destroyers of the old decrepit regime, unconditionally ruinous for all laboring people, and creators of a new, brighter future."[16]

When the Tsarist government decided in 1896 to close down the work of the Petersburg Committee for Literacy and to transform it into a more conservative organization, Rubakin, together with A. M. Kalmykova and V. V. Devel, turned to Tolstoy for a statement. The master addressed his answer to Kalmykova and referred to all three as "liberals," which in this context meant persons who had attempted to carry out social reform within the framework of the legal institutions of the Tsarist regime.

Tolstoy's answer constituted a major expression of his concept of passive resistance, or rather "non-resistance by force to evil." He rejected what he saw as the alternative lines of action followed by opponents of the regime: working within legal institutions or resorting to force to overthrow the regime. On the one hand, the government, ever alert to its own needs, would never tolerate the education of the masses; those, moreover, who chose to work within the system would hopelessly compromise their ultimate purposes in the interest of fleeting compromises. On the other hand, those taking recourse in violence were only laying the basis for violence against themselves: "A new order of things, established by force, would have to be continually supported by the same force. . . and it would ineluctably soon deteriorate just as that which it replaced."

In order to have the strength to resist, one must establish one's base: "In order to defend a fortress successfully, it is necessary to burn all the houses of the suburbs and to leave only that which is hard and which we are in no way inclined to yield." This would mean participating in no governmental institutions, refusing to serve as teachers or to send children to governmental schools, refusing to swear loyalty to the Tsar, and resisting the established church. The government, Tolstoy insisted, can punish crime and rebellion, but it can only create martyrs if it resorts to the use of force against passive resistance. "Only a person living according to his conscience," Tolstoy concluded, "can have a good influence on people."[17]

The letter had its impact on Rubakin. Not so much immediately, for Rubakin participated yet in terrorist activities, but after about a decade, Rubakin looked back at Tolstoy's words with more understanding and sympathy. In his *Sredi knig* he presented Tolstoy's new ideas as the major development in Russian intellectual history of the 1890s, and in later years he repeatedly declared that Tolstoy had been correct in asserting "that the most successful and most effective means of changing the existing structure consists in rejecting all forms of violence by man against man."[18]

As a self-proclaimed revolutionary, Rubakin was always a bit uncomfortable in noting that Tolstoy had referred to him as a "liberal," but in fact he maintained rather close relations with a number of liberals and "legal" Marxists. As his son has noted, Rubakin never truly became a "professional revolutionary." In his literary and educational work, he could be considered revolutionary, but by his dedication to books and to the spread of literacy, he had committed himself also to working within the system. Personally he was never so fully "magnetized" as he liked to picture himself, but neither did he become "demagnetized." Generally associated with the Socialist Revolutionaries, he had little contact with the villages; he was closer to the industrial workers, but he was not a Marxist. At the same time, he worked closely with liberals such as Paul N. Miliukov.[19]

Rubakin first met Miliukov in 1892 or 1893; they became better acquainted in Riazan in 1896; and they worked together closely until 1903. Writing in 1922, Rubakin declared that at one time Miliukov had represented "the voice of the whole Russian people." Miliukov, according to Rubakin, had made a great contribution to Russia through his efforts to further the education of the Russian intelligentsia. Miliukov had been the moving force in establishing the Commission for Home Reading, an organization which in effect became a university by correspondence, offering a total of four years of directed reading in all university disciplines but the applied sciences. This contributed greatly, Rubakin argued, to the development of the revolutionary intelligentsia in Russia between 1893 and 1917: "Even Miliukov's most outspoken enemies and opponents should be ready to pardon him all his 'sins' in their view for this one service of his to Russian civilization."[20]

A more sinister person with whom Rubakin became associated in this period was the agent provocateur Evno Azef. Rubakin was indignant when in 1917 a Petrograd newspaper published a secret police report which claimed that Rubakin had been among the first to suspect Azef "although he had essentially no evidence for this." Rubakin insisted that he had indeed had definite evidence.

Azef was the head of the "fighting section" of the Socialist Revolutionary Party, that is, its terrorist wing, and in this post he enjoyed a reputation as a bold tactician, fearing nothing. Rubakin first came into contact with him in 1903, and he helped Azef in making certain contacts. He also became suspicious of him almost immediately. Rubakin disliked Azef personally. Azef, he declared, sought only power, women, money, and luxury. Once, Rubakin charged, after having delivered a certain revolutionary to the police for execution, Azef hurried to Switzerland to comfort the grieving widow. Rubakin later produced a scornful physical description of Azef: "His eyes, gestures, and smiles were those of an accomplished scoundrel, not of a revolutionary. A round head, narrow forehead, staring eyes, the lower jaw of an animal, the thick lips of a depraved sybarite, ruddy cheeks bulging from an abundance of fat, thick arms, a round belly, broad, square shoulders, rather tall—this Azef was repulsive." His body, Rubakin continued, was "that of a cannibal. To the depth of its soul it was saturated with human blood—and with filth."

Rubakin's suspicions of Azef developed one day when Rubakin returned home to find that the papers in his study had been disturbed. Azef had been alone in the study, and Rubakin suspected that he had been looking for something. He began to watch the terrorist more carefully. Later a worker came to Rubakin's estranged wife and offered to expose a police agent. Rubakin paid 25 rubles for the service, and he found that Azef was the person in question. Rubakin took the information to the leadership of the Socialist Revolutionary Party, which in turn confronted Azef with the evidence. According to Rubakin, Azef then began to sob like an "hysterical woman," pointing to his record of assassinations. Over Rubakin's protests, the party leadership dropped the investigation.[21]

In the early 1900s, in addition to the general social and political tensions, Rubakin felt new pressures also in his personal life. Political repression struck hard at him, as he endured two searches and two deportations in three years. In 1902, as a member of a group of intellectuals protesting police actions against a crowd in front of the Kazan cathedral in St. Petersburg, he was exiled from the capital for a year, which time he spent in the Crimea.

At this time, Rubakin's marriage also was breaking up. Estranged from his wife even before his exile, Rubakin made their divorce final in 1904. The younger of their two sons joined his mother, the older, Alexander, remained with his father.

In the spring of 1903 Rubakin made a trip abroad with the woman who was eventually to become his second wife, Liudmila Alexandrovna Kilomiitseva. In the course of his travels, Rubakin became acquainted with western Switzerland, and in particular he stayed a while in Clarens, near Montreux, where he met George V. Plekhanov, the father of Russian Marxism. The combination of factors which he found in this region—the warm climate, the vigorous intellectual life of the Russian emigres living there, and the relatively inexpensive cost of living—all played a part in his eventual decision to settle there when he chose to emigrate in 1907. The warm climate may have been especially important in that he was a hypochondriac who constantly complained about his health but who also had continuing problems related to his having contracted nephritis in the 1890s.

In January 1904, after his return to St. Petersburg, Rubakin again brought the wrath of the authorities on his head. Addressing the Third Congress of Workers in Technical and Professional Education, he sought to encourage the development of alternative educational programs. To a certain degree echoing Tolstoy's letter of 1896, he argued that the official educational system was tendentious, aimed at producing useful citizens; the system was "nothing more than a weapon in the hands of the government for the realization of known, practical aims, closely connected with the interests of those social, economic, and political groups of which the state, at any given time, is the expression."[22]

Two days after this address, police officials came to Rubakin's home and searched the premises. Rubakin was ill, and the authorities took Liudmila Alexandrovna into custody for several days. She was finally informed that Rubakin would be sentenced to five years' exile in Siberia or that he might possibly be deported from Russia without the right to return. With testimony from a sympathetic doctor, Rubakin succeeded in winning deportation. He again traveled to Switzerland, and in the fall of 1904, after the assassination of the Minister of the Interior, Count von Plehve, the judgment was rescinded. Rubakin immediately returned to Russia, and in the winter of 1904-1905, he participated actively in support of the workers' movement headed by Father George Gapon, which culminated in the bloody events of Sunday, January 9, 1905.[23]

During the hectic year of 1905 Rubakin continued his literary work, compiling the first edition of his recommendatory bibliography, *Sredi knig*, a listing of 7000 Russian books in all subjects. In June his mother died. When his son Alexander was arrested in January 1906, Rubakin became even more concerned about the future, although his son was promptly released. Fearing the consequences of his own connections with the Socialist Revolutionaries, he moved to Finland in May 1906; there he felt somewhat more secure. In August Liudmila Alexandrovna bore him a son.

In the summer of 1906, however, Alexander was again arrested, and Rubakin now turned seriously to thoughts of emigrating from Russia. He had to resolve a number of problems first, not the least of which was the fate of his library, which he now measured as extending one verst, 240 sazhens, and nine inches, or almost one mile (5250 feet and nine inches).[24] He was opposed in principle to selling his books, and therefore he chose to donate the collection to the All-Russian League for Education. He kept some 7000 books for himself, and he made arrangement with a friend for their shipment once he had settled in Switzerland.

In November 1907 he departed from Russia for the last time, with, it might be noted, a legal passport.[25] When Alexander Nikolaevich escaped from exile and came to Finland in December, he obtained a false passport and followed his father to Geneva.

III   IN THE EMIGRATION

By 1907 a large Russian colony had already established itself in Switzerland. The Swiss census of 1910 reported 4525 women and 3933 men as giving Russian as their native language. The largest settlements of Russians included 2155 persons in Zurich, 2107 in Geneva, 865 in Lausanne, 720 in Bern, and 545 in Basel.

Many of these had come as students; one-fourth to one-third of them attended Swiss universities at any given time. In 1907 Russian citizens represented 34.2% of the total enrollment at the seven Swiss universities, and the 1311 Russians studying medicine constituted 70% of the enrollment in Switzerland's five medical schools. The 1454 Russian women at the universities made up the majority of the female students at these institutions.[1]

The Swiss prided themselves on their hospitality toward political emigres from other lands, but by the beginning of the twentieth century, they had begun to watch their guests more carefully. A bombing incident in Zurich in 1889 led to greater control over Russian students, and three years later the Zurich police established a Fremdenbureau which centralized the granting of residence permits throughout the entire canton. Recurring complaints arose about Russian students crowding the universities, and the Federal Council, the Bundesrat, expressed concerns about disease and crime among the Russians. Nevertheless, although the University of Zurich had quietly established a quota by 1914, Russian political emigres continued to find haven in the country. Every March, the Swiss Socialist Party solicited contributions for aid to Russian political prisoners and exiles, and in the summer of 1914, the various aid organizations in Switzerland combined to form the "League of Swiss Relief Societies for Political Prisoners and Exiles of Russia."[2]

For their part, the emigres generally found Switzerland hospitable. They welcomed the opportunity to discuss their political philosophies relatively freely, and one veteran Bolshevik revolutionary even spoke of "Switzerland's monopoly in the free expression of revolutionary thoughts."[3] Another Bolshevik praised the accomplishments of the

Swiss: "Diligently working and sincerely helping one another, the Swiss have achieved an order and prosperity to which other larger states are still only striving. Switzerland is going ahead of all of them."[4] Rubakin's son lauded the honesty of the Swiss, although he noted that some Russian emigres considered this honesty "depressing."[5]

The Russians included a number of distinguished figures, but for the most part they kept aloof from the mainstream of Swiss society. To be sure, in Geneva Jacques Dicker, a Socialist Revolutionary who came to Switzerland in 1906, eventually became a leading figure in radical Swiss politics; Naum Reichesberg, a native of Kiev, became Professor Ordinarius for Statistics and Political Economy at the University of Bern in 1906; and in Zurich, Paul Axelrod, a veteran Russian socialist, started a yogurt business which still bears his name. For each such man, however, there were dozens who, like George Plekhanov, Vladimir Lenin, or Vera Figner, looked upon themselves as exiles who would yet return to Russia. Rubakin, for example, lived forty years in Switzerland without taking Swiss citizenship.

Upon arriving in Switzerland, Rubakin traveled first to Geneva, where he found a place in a school run by Ivan Ivanovich Fidler for the children of Russian emigres. (Among the staff was Catherine Peshkova, the first wife of the writer Maxim Gorky.) Rubakin's son Alexander soon joined him, and he looked around for suitable housing which could contain the new library which he planned to assemble.

He eventually found a five-story building in Baugy-sur-Clarens, a suburb of Montreux on the eastern shore of the Lake of Geneva. He took both apartments on the top floor, each consisting of five bright rooms with central heating. Now he sent for his books from Finland, and at the age of 46 he launched a new career.[6]

Rubakin now proceeded with the assembling of his second library. Even though now in Switzerland, he was able to maintain close contact with the Russian world of books. Publishers sent him review copies of their new works, and authors sent him their newest books. His own publishers, including Prometei, E. D. Trautskaia, Posrednik, Prosveshchenie, and others, sent him copies of their publications as part of his author's royalties. He also arranged on occasion to exchange copies of his works with other publishers. This drew protests from his publishers on occasion, but he persisted in this practice. For Rubakin the issue was to acquire books as simply and as cheaply as possible.[7]

Rubakin's collection quickly became a major link in the network of Russian libraries in Switzerland. Many of these were only small collections, such as the Russisches Leseverein in Zurich or the Bibliotheque Russe in Lausanne. Others were relatively large, such as the Leo

Tolstoy library in Geneva, which, when turned over to the Bibliotheque Publique et Universitaire in 1918, numbered some 18,000 volumes. Another important collection was the Bolshevik library in Geneva, organized by G. A. Kuklin and in 1908 taken over by V. A. Karpinsky. Kuklin handled the details on the Swiss side in shipping Rubakin's books from Finland, and Karpinsky exchanged duplicates with Rubakin and also sought his advice on purchases.[8]

Rubakin's home also became an important waystation for Russian intellectuals fleeing Russia or even simply traveling in the West. As he described it, "Through our apartments annually came not even dozens but hundreds of fellow nationals, coming to us for information, explanations, advice, and aid of all sorts."[9]

Immediately upon settling in Baugy, Rubakin became a part of the older generation of Russian emigres. A particularly close friend was E. E. Lazarev, who in the 1870s had been a member of the "Zemlia i volia" organization.[10] Twice imprisoned by Tsarist authorities, Lazarev was an old acquaintance of Leo Tolstoy's and had even served as a prototype for one of the figures in the novel *Resurrection*. In the early 1900s he had settled in Baugy, where he operated a small dairy farm.

Another frequent visitor to Rubakin's home was Vera Figner, who had come to Switzerland after completing her 25 years of imprisonment in Schlusselberg prison. Figner, together with Lazarev and others, often participated in musical evenings at Rubakin's home, which featured the piano playing of Rubakin's wife, Liudmila Alexandrovna.[11]

Curiously, Rubakin's library attracted a great number of Bolsheviks, including A. A. Troianovsky, A. V. Lunacharsky, N. N. Krylenko, G. A. Alexinsky, and later D. Z. Manuilsky.[12] Of these, Anatole Lunacharsky became a particularly close friend, although the two had many arguments about Lunacharsky's cavalier physical treatment of books. Lunacharsky marked up books heavily in reading them, and Rubakin objected strongly to this practice. Nevertheless, Rubakin, while calling Lunacharsky "not a serious person," respected his broad erudition.[13]

G. V. Plekhanov found Rubakin's library invaluable in his preparation of a history of Russian social thought. Now essentially removed from the revolutionary political scene, Plekhanov was dedicating his efforts to a scholarly presentation of his interpretation of history.[14] In an essay which he later wrote about Plekhanov, Rubakin took special note of Plekhanov's militant Marxism. Plekhanov, he declared, always looked in the books he read for things to confirm his political beliefs. As for Plekhanov's renowned belligerent nature, Rubakin noted that he was a "fighting man. Disputes and struggle were his element." An expert in polemic, Plekhanov knew how to infuriate his opponents, and he did so deliberately, as a tactic. At the same time, Plekhanov was a "convinced anti-terrorist"; he could hate, Rubakin declared, "but hate principles, not people." Above all, Rubakin was impressed by Plekhanov's dedication: "Seldom can one meet people who can so love their work as Plekhanov loved his."[15]

Rubakin also learned to know Plekhanov as a fallible human being. In March 1914 Plekhanov, in response to Rubakin's complaints that some books had been damaged in the mail, insisted that one had already been torn when he received it. Nevertheless, he was ready to pay for the damage: "I do not know how to thank you for your goodness, and I do not want to abuse it."[16] In 1909 Plekhanov once had to apologize for not having sent Rubakin a copy of one of his books: "My wife is at our cottage, and without her I cannot find any of my publications."[17]

Plekhanov and Rubakin worked together closely and respected each other, but they did not become friends. Plekhanov gave Rubakin considerable help in the preparation of the second edition of *Sredi knig,* and Rubakin waived his own rule against sending books outside of the Montreax region as he supplied Plekhanov's needs. In 1912, when Rubakin announced his own twenty-fifth anniversary as a writer, Plekhanov wrote, "I hasten to congratulate you, whom writing has certainly provided many happy minutes, and also to congratulate Russian literature (this latter, however, only mentally), which has, in your person, such a talented, honest, and industrious worker." At another time, while working on his history of Russian social thought, Plekhanov wrote, "I sometimes say to myself, 'I hope that Nikolai Alexandrovich will approve of my work.' In truth your praise will be a fine reward for me." In the forward to his history, Plekhanov gave special thanks to Rubakin, and upon receiving the first three copies of his second volume from the publisher, he immediately sent one to Rubakin with his compliments.[18]

When Lenin came to Switzerland in the fall of 1914, he too visited Rubakin, who arranged a special meeting at his apartment at which the Bolshevik leader spoke. Rubakin was apparently never well inclined toward Lenin, although he recognized the strength of the man. In an essay published in 1918, he characterized Lenin as a man of "willpower and emotion." As a man of will power, "he not only fought but he did so bitterly"; as a man of emotion, "he is capable of exaggerated love and exaggerated hate." Above all Lenin hated the bourgeoisie: "His hatred directs itself, however, not against people but a system." Rubakin even considered that Lenin hated the bourgeoisie more than he loved the proletariat. Lenin was "in essence a despot." In his thoughts politics "unconditionally dominated ethics." Eventually, Rubakin predicted, Lenin would go the way of Robespierre.[19]

For all his association with leading Russian revolutionaries, Rubakin during this time was becoming increasingly apolitical. His disillusionment with the Socialist Revolutionary Party in connection with the Azef affair, combined with his increasing interest in the thoughts of Tolstoy, led him toward a new outlook on life. He cooperated with Vladimir Burtsev in the latter's campaign to expose Azef,[20] and after the provocateur had been discredited, Rubakin withdrew from the Socialist Revolutionary Party.

Writing in 1922, Rubakin declared, "The history of all possible, often contradictory opinions destroyed in me any dogmatism—social, philosophical, or scientific—leaving for me only an ethical dogmatism."[21] Six years later he commented, "I am not one of those who has already found the truth, but one of whose who seek and to the end of their days will seek it. Therefore I will never feel myself capable of belonging to any party; for me it is enough that from the very beginning of my literary, scientific, and public activity, I have not changed my world outlook and my decidedly socialist revolutionary attitude toward the old regime, and I am never about to change it."[22] From 1909 on, he insisted on calling himself a "supraparty socialist."

Testimony on Rubakin's withdrawal from politics was offered even by the agents of the Okhrana, the Tsarist secret police. On May 31, 1910, the Ministry of Internal Affairs ordered the Paris agency of the Okhrana to investigate a rumor that Rubakin was planning to organize libraries in Russian villages and to distribute Socialist Revolutionary literature. Two weeks later the Paris office reported that Rubakin was "far from any party matters," and that he was taking no part in the activities of the Socialist Revolutionary Party. Declaring that Rubakin would engage in no enterprise which would not bring him some financial return, the report commented, "Although at the present time, Rubakin, according to our information, is working on a bibliographical work in the spirit of the Socialist Revolutionary Party, nevertheless this work has a purely literary character and is not meant for purposes of propaganda."[23]

The Okhrana's report accurately touched on both of Rubakin's major concerns in this period: his literary work and his need to raise money. Personally Rubakin was anything but profligate. According to his son, Rubakin wore the same suit and overcoat for ten years. But that same son was now studying medicine in Paris, and Rubakin sent him one hundred francs per month, a sum which still failed to cover Alexander Nikolaevich's expenses.[24] For Rubakin, however, this represented a large sum and a drain on his library's resources.

Despite his physical isolation in Switzerland, Rubakin remained in close touch with the Russian book trade. Before he left Finland, he had contacted several publishers on the question of giving one the right to his collected works. It was a difficult time for publishers, and in March 1907 Granat rejected his proposal.[25] In April, Z. Nikitin of Prosveshchenie complained, "The situation in the book market is now very bad; even the good books are not moving."[26] By the end of the year, conditions had improved to the point that Prosveshchenie was ready to negotiate with Rubakin, and in January 1908 it offered him a royalty of fifteen percent of the selling price of the books. Rubakin countered with a demand for nine kopecs per signature, a royalty which would come to about twice Prosveshchenie's offer. On March 5, 1908, Prosveshchenie's representative, N. S. Tsetlin, rejected Rubakin's demands as offensive and unjust.[27]

Rubakin persisted, turning to other publishers with his various projects. In March 1908 A. F. Marks turned down Rubakin's proposal for a second edition of *Sredi knig*, and Prosveshchenie rejected it in April.[28] In 1909 Ksenofont Tikhomirov expressed a readiness to publish *Sredi knig* in an edition of 3000 copies, paying a royalty of 1350 rubles, but Rubakin wanted both a larger printing and a larger royalty.[29] He finally agreed to give the work to the firm Nauka, headed by Ivan Borisovich Pozdeev.

Rubakin and Pozdeev quickly reached an agreement whereby Pozdeev promised a royalty of 3000 rubles, of which he paid one-third immediately, on an edition of 5000 copies. Rubakin spoke of the new edition as "thoroughly reworked, supplemented, brought up to date, and transformed into a practical and theoretical guide for the selection of books generally. . . and for book stores and libraries in particular."[30] He spoke glowingly of having the first 7000 of the 20,000 titles already in order, but he was in fact referring only to the listing of titles in the first edition. It remained yet for him to write preliminary comments for each of the separate subjects in the bibliography. This was to prove an enormous job, far greater than either Rubakin or Pozdeev had imagined. Instead of 500-600 pages as first conceived, the work as published, even though incomplete, extended to more than 1700 pages.

Pozdeev had hoped that the book would be ready to go on the market by May of 1910, but Rubakin countered with the view that it should be the first item in a new season, that is, it should appear in September.[31] Rubakin proved incapable of meeting even his own schedule, and an increasing burden of mediating between author and publisher fell upon the editor of the volume, I. V. Gulbinsky, himself a capable bibliographer who published under the name of I. Vladislavlev.[32] Besides sympathizing with both sides, Gulbinsky had to filter Pozdeev's outbursts over the slow progress of the work and also to spur Rubakin on to work more quickly.[33]

In the fall of 1910 Pozdeev yielded to the realities of the situation and agreed to Rubakin's proposal that the work be issued in separate volumes. Even so, only by employing extraordinary pressures and tactics, such as refusing to send page proofs to Rubakin, could Gulbinsky bring the first volume into the world at the beginning of May 1911.[34]

The first volume listed over 6500 books, divided among the classifications of belles lettres, dramatic arts, journalism, and "ethics or the science of morals and ideals." Although Rubakin had repeatedly insisted that the book was to serve as a guide for self-education, the very sight of facing pages which contained almost seventy lines of small print without indentations for new paragraphs had to discourage all but the most enterprising and intrepid readers. Nevertheless it received generally favorable reviews, and Rubakin collected great praise, albeit no financial reward. Pozdeev insisted that his firm had to recover its costs before he could resume payment of the royalty. Since the original advance had long since been spent, Rubakin had to finish the work with his own resources.

Rubakin attempted to raise money by turning to other enterprises. In March 1910 Prosveshchenie proposed renewing negotiations on the publication of Rubakin's collected works on the basis of its earlier offer of a fifteen percent royalty. This time Rubakin agreed, but at the beginning of 1911 Prosveshchenie had trouble with Tsarist censors in connection with another author. Therefore it proposed to Rubakin that any of his works which might have such trouble be published by another firm. Prosveshchenie would vouch for the firm chosen. When Rubakin objected, negotiations again came to a halt.[35]

In dealing with emigres, Rubakin regularly insisted that he too was a political emigre. In dealing with publishers who feared censorship, however, he sounded a different note: "Not one of my books has been confiscated or banned," he wrote to Ksenofont Tikhomirov. He insisted that he was in Switzerland "not as an emigre but as a sick man. I even have a document from the consulate to the effect that my reentry into Russia is not at all forbidden." At the same time, he admitted, "I have already lost the feeling as to what the censor there in Russia considers permissible and what not."[36]

For all his protestations, Rubakin knew well that his works were drawing the fire of conservative forces in Russia. A publication of the Union of the Archangel Michael, reissued several times between 1907 and 1914, chose Rubakin as a special target in its criticisms of textbooks in Russian schools. "Rubakin," it declared, "is the purest atheist and anarchist. This is of course his affair. But how was his book *Among*

29

Mysteries and Miracles, prepared for children of school age, passed for publication and distribution?" The publication called the distribution of Rubakin's works among students "a serious crime of the Ministry of National Education."[37] A journal published by the union described Rubakin as "anarchist, positivist, and atheist."[38]

Despite such attacks, Rubakin still succeeded in finding publishers. Tikhomirov accepted several works, especially ones on popular scientific topics. Tikhomirov also published Rubakin's translations of the works of the Franch geographer Elisee Reclus; for this alone Rubakin received 1600 francs.[39]

In June 1911 the firm Mir invited Rubakin to edit a series of children's books on the "continuous struggle and heroic efforts of mankind" in the area of discoveries in the natural sciences. As he entered into negotiations with Mir, Rubakin turned to Plekhanov for advice, and the latter advised him to accept the offer: "These terms are more favorable than those on which I work for Mir." Mir, Plekhanov continued, was an honorable firm: "It apparently does not deceive like other publishers. You cannot imagine how I have suffered, and indeed now suffer, from this fraternity."[40]

In November 1911 Prosveshchenie came back with another proposal for the publication of Rubakin's works. Despite Rubakin's eagerness for an agreement, difficulties still arose. Continuing to fear censorship, Prosveshchenie insisted that it would accept only books on nature and geography. In January 1912 N. S. Tsetlin insisted that Rubakin had agreed to give "all your works, the new and also those already in print, exclusively to us for publication from now on." Rubakin was eventually able to straighten out the confusion, limiting his obligation to Prosveshchenie, but Tsetlin was yet to complain that the titles which Rubakin was offering for reprinting were still in stock with other publishers.[41]

Desperately trying to raise new money to underwrite his long-standing projects, Rubakin had overextended himself. Complicating his situation still more was a protracted illness in the winter of 1911-1912. Pozdeev and Gulbinsky pressed him relentlessly for manuscript of *Sredi knig,* and in April 1912 Mir began to complain that he had not yet delivered a publication plan for the series of children's books.[42] At the same time, Tsetlin argued that while Prosveshchenie did not mean to challenge Rubakin's credibility, it had not yet received anything in return for its payment of some 2000 rubles to Rubakin.[43] In July even Tikhomirov declared that he could not give Rubakin advances on his anticipated royalties.[44]

Rubakin also had trouble with his old friend I. D. Sytin. Sytin's newspaper *Russkoe Slovo* had been carrying a column by Rubakin entitled "Among Books and Readers." For his efforts here Rubakin had been receiving both an honorarium and free books. In the summer of 1912, Sytin liquidated the column. Rubakin protested vainly that while Russian reactionaries were attacking him personally, Sytin had had no problems with censorship on account of the column. Sytin's action now left him in difficult financial straits.[45]

In August, Mir, having received Rubakin's plan for the children's series, complained that the books would be too complicated even for adults. In September the firm refused to pay Rubakin any more money until the series began publication.[46]

Rubakin's troubles continued on into the winter of 1912-1913. After complaining that Rubakin had not offered any works for publication, Prosveshchenie then began to express concern that he was seeking to increase the number of illustrations in the works which he was now submitting in order to raise his own royalty. By the end of the year, the firm had paid Rubakin over 5000 rubles as advances; in its concern for obtaining more titles, it even declared itself ready to accept historical works, provided they could pass the censorship which was especially "burdensome" at this time.[47]

Mir now complained that Rubakin was planning to make the children's books too large. This would hinder selling subscriptions to the series, and the company declared that in no case would it increase Rubakin's royalties. When the first manuscript arrived, the firm complained that while it was written with "your usual talent," it seemed to be written for slow adults rather than for children.[48] In this case, Rubakin admitted failure and notified the firm that he could not live up to the contract. The company expressed shock but declared that it did not exploit its authors: "Naturally we free you from the obligations undertaken toward us."[49]

A new problem arose for Rubakin with the ratification in August 1912 of a publishing convention between France and Russia. This severely hampered his profitable practice of reworking popular French works for the Russian market. When Rubakin wrote to the French historian Charles Seignobos concerning rights to his *History of Civilization*, the latter referred him to his publishers. As Rubakin later informed Dmitry Ksenofonovich Tikhomirov, the terms proposed proved to be too high.[50]

In the spring of 1913, the second volume of *Sredi knig* finally reached completion, and it appeared early in the fall. For help with the preparation of this volume, Rubakin had recruited many of the leading figures on the Russian intellectual and revolutionary scene. Plekhanov and the anarchist Peter Kropotkin read sections; N. I. Kareev and V. I. Semevsky read the historical sections; Naum Reichesberg helped with the section on statistics; and Julius Martov and Lenin contributed brief descriptions of their respective programs for Russian Social Democracy. Totalling over 900 pages, the volume listed books in the social sciences, history, government, education, philosophy, and economics. Like the first volume, this one had again cost all the principals dear. Responding to Rubakin's clmplaints about his personal sacrifices in preparing the work, Gulbinsky pointed out that he too had made sacrifices. Rubakin repentantly answered, "The appearance of *Sredi knig,* I repeat, owes as much to you as to me." A whimsical postscript to another of Bulbinsky's letters read, "Greetings on the appearance of the second volume, in the preparation of which I too played a certain role"—it was signed by Gulbinsky's wife.[51]

Like the first volume, the second volume won generally favorable reviews. In a commentary which Soviet writers have considered a fundamental work in the development of Soviet bibliographical practices, Lenin asserted that *Sredi knig"*s shortcomings lay in the author's "electicism" and in his failure to seek enough aid from specialists. Lenin curtly dismissed Rubakin's claims of objectivity and of standing above party conflict as being in fact a "concealed polemic," which was more dangerous than open polemics. Nevertheless he considered the work generally successful; uttering words which every author longs to hear, Lenin declared, "No substantial library can manage without Rubakin's works."[52]

In the last year before World War I, Rubakin worked feverishly on the third volume of *Sredi knig,* which was to contain sections on the national question, geography, and psychology, as well as an index of authors, an index of reviews, and a bibliographical section. He devoted special attention to the section on the nationalities of Russia; his interest, however, was drifting away from an interpretation of the national question from a socialist point of view and more toward a study of each national movement. This trend was reflected by the fact that he relied less on Plekhanov now and he developed new contacts among emigres from the various national minorities of the Tsarist Empire.

Sredi knig required prodigious effort, but it brought little financial return. Far more successful in this sense was Rubakin's continuing program for studying and corresponding with the Russian reading public. He published questionnaires in several journals, inviting readers to write to him concerning their needs and desires, and then he would draw up individualized programs for self-education and offer advice on the selection of books. From 1911 to 1915 he corresponded with a total of 5507 readers.[53] In turn he published excerpts from this correspondence, and these books were among his most profitable ventures in this period. In all, Rubakin found life in the emigration difficult. Always financially troubled, fearing illness, he had to struggle to maintain his library. He was having increasing difficulty meeting his past obligations, and publishers were showing ever greater hesitance in accepting his new proposals. It would appear that his relations with Russian publishers would have soon reached the point of crisis even without the coming of war. Irascible and proud, he used harsh words in dealing with his publishers; he complained frequently of mistreatment.[54] It would seem that in fact he had overextended himself.

The preparation of *Sredi knig* took a heavy toll, both financially and physically, but this work was to stand as Rubakin's greatest accomplishment. In 1914 he probably did not realize this. He was just 52 years old, and he had greater aspirations yet. War and revolution were to change his world entirely.

IV   WORLD WAR I

When the First World War began in August 1914, it brought confusion and eventually new divisions to the Russian emigres in Western Europe. After a first surge of sympathy and even enthusiasm for the cause of the Entente, strong anti-war feelings developed within the emigration. By the fall of 1915, the emigres were rather sharply divided into three groups: the "defensists" advocated support of the war effort against the Central Powers; the "internationalists" called for an end to the war on the basis of "no annexations, no indemnities"; and the "defeatists" expressed their readiness to countenance the defeat of Russia in their efforts to convert the war into revolution.[1]

In Switzerland, which remained neutral, the emigres were of course not threatened by the war, but they found themselves cut off from all communication with Russia. For many, such as Rubakin, this meant being cut off from sources of funds. Over 500 persons took advantage of the possibility of returning to Russia on a ship leaving Genoa in September.[2]

Mutual aid groups arose throughout Switzerland. In Zurich emigres organized a Committee of Social Salvation, which operated a communal kitchen in the quarters of the Union of Russian Students. By the middle of August it was serving meals to 150 persons, barely half of whom had the money to pay for the food.[3] In Bern, in November, representatives of Russian colonies throughout Switzerland met with officials of the Imperial mission and named Naum Reichesberg as president of the Central Committee for Aid to Russian Citizens. In a letter to Rubakin, Reichesberg characterized the panic among the emigres during August and September as "black days."[4]

Rubakin's entry in his diary for August 6, 1914, read, "I predict: Russia will be beaten. France and England will defeat the Germans. Austria will break up, as will Russia. The Romanov dynasty is finished."[5] Personally, Rubakin ranged himself with the internationalists, although he often took a virtually defeatist position. Lenin's characterization of him as a "defensist" in 1917 probably had more to do with his growing pacifism than with his feelings about the Tsarist government.[6]

In September 1914, working with Lazarev and Boris Chlenov, another veteran emigre who was a *docent* at the University of Bern, Rubakin helped to organize a Russian Club in Montreux. The three men conceived of this group as a discussion club, rather than a mutual aid society such as those springing up among Russians in other Swiss cities. They decreed that only tea could be drunk; they banned wine and card-playing. As Rubakin described it, the group organized a "general conference of known mutual enemies," an "educational establishment absolutely nonparty or, more exactly speaking, above party."[7]

These efforts met with mixed reaction. For one, Vera Figner, who took a defensist position, would have nothing to do with it. As she wrote to Rubakin's wife, Rubakin was "naturally indignant because of my nonparticipation in the Russian Club, but I expect nothing good from it. Yet if I am wrong I will be happy."[8] From Bern, on the other hand, Reichesberg asked for news of the club's activity, noting that it had been impossible to do anything of that sort in the Swiss capital.[9]

In its first two months of operation, the club held ten meetings, five of which included musical programs organized by Liudmila Alexandrovna. Among the speakers were Plekhanov, Constantine Oberuchev, and Gregory Alexinsky, all supporting the war effort, and Paul Biriukov, Lenin, Nikolai Krylenko, and Rubakin, all speaking in opposition to the war.

Gatherings which included presentation of such mutually antagonistic views soon became impossible in the heated atmosphere of World War I, but in the fall of 1914 they played an important role in the new political differentiation among the emigres. Until Plekhanov gave a public lecture in Lausanne on October 11, many emigres doubted that he had indeed uttered the statements which the Entente press had attributed to him. In Lausanne he confirmed the reports; he was an outspoken supporter of the war effort against Germany. "Plekhanov's speech was horrible," wrote Biriukov to Rubakin.[10] Plekhanov made a similar presentation the next day to the Russian Club in Montreux and then refrained from further public appearances.

When Lenin spoke at a meeting of the club in the Hotel Splendid on October 26, his appearance drew a crowd of more than 200 persons. This was not just a gathering of Russians, however; Rubakin later wrote of the presence of a "hotel public" which "came not to hear the speaker but to see him." Lenin, who had first publicized his views on the war in a commentary after Plekhanov's speech in Lausanne, apparently shocked his audience by calling for the defeat of Tsarist Russia.[11]

As the emigres now formed new alliances and old friendships

dissolved, Rubakin somehow managed to maintain his broad network of friends and contacts. He himself took an internationalist stance, but the defensists continued to come to him. Plekhanov sent him a copy of his brochure on the war, *La social-democratie et la guerre*, and, in sending a copy of his history of Russian social thought, he explained that the introduction to the work contained "my philosophy of the 'revolution' of 1905-1906. Whoever knows this philosophy of history will understand also my tactical line. I would especially want this to be clear to you."[12]

The most prominent and outspoken of the defensists among the Russian socialists was Gregory Alexinsky, a former Bolshevik and now an implacable foe of Lenin. Alexinsky had played a part in the founding of the Russian Club, but he soon dedicated his efforts to investigating and exposing German machinations among the emigres. Although Rubakin himself entered into contacts with the Germans in 1915, Alexinsky continued to correspond with him thorughout the war. In May 1915 he requested details about the activities of certain Ukrainian agents in Switzerland, and in June he proudly wrote of the anger which he had aroused. As late as the fall of 1916 and the beginning of 1917 Alexinsky still wrote with news of Rubakin's son Alexander, who served in the French army and who was working with the defensist publication *Russkaia Volia*, printed in Paris.[13]

Rubakin also maintained relations for a while with the Tsarist mission in Bern. Because of the breakdown in communications with Russia at the beginning of the war, Rubakin had to turn to the mission for aid in obtaining his money from publishers. Even here he could find a public. In the fall of 1915, V. M. Felkner, an employee of the embassy who specialized in dealing with emigres, sent Rubakin some books with the comment, "However few of these publications are sent to me, I consider myself obliged to pass on at least one copy of them to the deeply revered author of *Sredi knig*."[14]

On the other extreme, the Bolsheviks continued to patronize his library. Lenin visited him on many of his trips to French Switzerland and also borrowed books by mail, although Rubakin's own records made no listing of this.[15]

The war brought many new readers to Rubakin in addition to his old clientele; Lenin's appearance in Montreux alone brought at least a dozen new readers. Ever studying the readers and their choices of books, Rubakin insisted that the growing demand for books confirmed his view that the influence of a book depended "not so much on its own quality as on the political and social characteristics of the readers."[16] Two of the most popular books in his collection at this time were Tolstoy's *War and Peace* and Paul Miliukov's *Balkanskii krizis*, a

study of the Bosnian crisis of 1908.[17]
Among the better known of Rubakin's new patrons were D. Z. Manuilsky and Felix Kon. Manuilsky, one of the founders of the internationalist Russian newspapers in Paris, *Golos* and *Nashe Slovo*, came to Switzerland in the fall of 1915 and asked Rubakin for aid in finding work. Curiously, he used Alexinsky as a reference even though the two, once friends, had now taken bitterly opposing views on the war.[18] Kon began by borrowing books and advising Rubakin concerning works on anthropology and on Polish nationalism; in the fall of 1916 he eagerly accepted an invitation to work as Rubakin's secretary.[19]

Not all Rubakin's visitors, however, were seeking books. As a major cultural center for revolutionary emigres, the library also attracted police agents, spies, and various other persons with special causes. In 1915 a German agent attempted in vain to find a job in the library.[20] Okhrana agents reported regularly on the activities at his establishment. In 1916 when Miliukov visited Western Europe as part of a Russian parliamentary delegation, he too made his way to Rubakin in order to learn of current developments within the Russian emigration.[21]

Rubakin's own work was deeply affected by the news in the spring of 1915 that Pozdeev had decided to publish the part of the third volume of *Sredi knig* which had been set up in type and to suspend any further work on the project for for the duration of the war. The volume appeared in April 1915 and included works on geography, ethnography, anthropology, and the national question. Rubakin now found himself free to turn to other projects.[22]

He now began to plan a large study of the Tsarist empire, tentatively entitled "Dve Rossii" (Two Russias). As a subtitle, Rubakin wrote, "The Russian sphinx and its riddle; Russia is not one but two." The Two Russias were represented by the government and the people. In analyzing the government, Rubakin outlined the following topics: the social and juridical bases of the autocracy, the results of autocracy, our backwardness, economic life, cultural-social life, the struggle with personal freedom and personal initiative, the struggle with social initiative and with self-government, spiritual life, and foreign policy.

In his outline for the discussion of the people, Rubakin listed: the significance of the peasantry, the population and its national composition; the toiling classes: peasants, factory workers, the service and intellectual proletariat; the bourgeois classes: landlords, industrialists, merchants, bureaucrats, the clergy, the military; what do peasants give and receive from society: food, schools; who pays and who benefits from taxes; who decides, and how, what is useful and necessary for the people; the lot of the peasantry: poverty and destitution, famines, disease, birth, and death.[23]

This work was obviously meant to sum up his various studies over Russian bureaucracy, the peasantry, and other aspects of Russian life. It also followed the general pattern of his statistical studies of Russia,[24] which still enjoyed broad use among the revolutionary intellectuals. Although Rubakin planned and plotted energetically to bring the study to fruition, however, he was never able to complete the manuscript. He later merged "Dve Rossii" into a larger project tentatively entitled "Tragediia russkogo naroda" (The Tragedy of the Russian People), which was in turn to become the first volume in a grand series on "The Renewal of Russian History." The project was never finished, and eventually parts of it were published as separate articles in various western periodicals.[25]

Rubakin may well have been behind the mysterious visitor who came to the German embassy in Bern in the summer of 1915. The German ambassador, Baron Gisbert von Romberg, reported that a visitor had proposed to publish a collection of "important and as yet unknown sensational documents" about Russia. Since the man expected large sales in America, he had requested only "modest financial help," together with a gurantee of asylum in either Germany or Austria-Hungary. The request for modest remuneration combined with visions of a large mass market was typical of Rubakin's proposals to publishers, although the inquiry about asylum seems rather uncharacteristic.[26]

At the same time, Rubakin was investigating still another new market for his literary and bibliographic efforts. By the fall of 1915, many Russian emigre groups in Switzerland were expressing great concern about the intellectual fate of the prisoners of war held by the Central Powers. Already in December 1914, Victor Chernov, a leading Socialist Revolutionary, had reportedly declared, "The prisoners are our army."[27] Various political groups, including the Bolsheviks and the Socialist Revolutionaries, soon organized their own communications with the prisoners, and a number of relief societies sprang into existence. In its fourth plenary meeting, held on September 30 and October 1, 1915, the Central Committee for Aid to Russian Citizens in Switzerland, chaired by Naum Reichesberg, offered aid to all socialist organizations in Switzerland helping the prisoners of war. It also expressed interest in a proposal by Rubakin for organizing libraries in the prison camps, and it named Rubakin and Constantine Oberuchev as its consultants on aid for the prisoners.[28]

Oberuchev, a retired colonel of artillery, had been exiled from Russia in 1914 for a period of three years. He had first met Rubakin, who was the same age as he, in 1886; "We dreamed together of creating a a military organization," he later reminded Rubakin. In 1907 Oberuchev had been forced to retire from the army because of his activites as a member of the Socialist Revolutionary Party. At the outbreak of the war, like many other emigres, he offered his service to his homeland, but he was refused. He then turned to relief work, and in resentment for what he considered the Russian government's neglect of the prisoners of war, he gradually made the transition to an internationalist position. It was he who carried Rubakin's proposal to the Central Committee.[29]

Reichesberg formally notified Rubakin of the Central Committee's decision on October 14, announcing, "The committee has instructed me to ask you to take on *all the tasks* of organizing the indicated matter." There was, however, little money, and Rubakin should avoid giving the project a "political and especially a party character, since the matter could suffer from this." The committee felt, Reichesberg concluded, "that no one could fulfill this task better than you."[30]

Rubakin willingly accepted the task, and in fact he had already entered into direct contact with Romberg on the question of organizing libraries in the camps. A Ukrainian, Vladimir Stepankowski, had mentioned Rubakin's name to Romberg in June, and in July he had described Rubakin's plan for a "bill of indictment" (*Anklageschrift*) against the Russian government, to be made up of secret diplomatic documents. Rubakin was also reportedly considering the publication of a newspaper for the prison camps.[31]

The German Auswartiges Amt immediately expressed a strong interest in working with Rubakin. Staatssekretar Arthur Zimmermann spoke of him as "a suitable force for anti-Russian propaganda,[32] but Stepankowski was unable to bring him in to meet Romberg. Romberg then sent Alexander Keskula, an emigre Estonian already in the pay of the Germans, to visit Rubakin, and on September 17 Keskula presented Rubakin's terms: aid in the publication of his indictment (presumably "Dve Rossii") and a guaranteed annual income of 12,500 francs. Keskula had a rather unfavorable impression of Rubakin: he had "an important name but no organization behind him." On another occasion, Keskula indicated a strong dislike for him: "I would really prefer to have nothing to do with the fellow—I hope soon to be in such a position."[33]

Rubakin was motivated to deal directly with the Germans by appeals which he was receiving directly from prisoners of war who remembered his name from the days before the war. A letter from the library committee of the prisoner camp in Hannover, Germany, dated August 19, 1915, reported that the camp held 1900 prisoners and expected to double in size in the course of the winter. The committee asked for Rubakin's help in obtaining books—belles lettres, popular scientific works, journals, newspapers, and textbooks in all branches of knowledge for "our school."[34]

On September 22 Rubakin met with Keskula, Romberg, and Carl von Schubert, the German Legationsrat. Rubakin proceeded to call German propaganda among the prisoners of war ineffective, and he proposed the establishment of small libraries of perhaps 600 books each at every camp. He asked 5000 to 10,000 francs for the task. His own works, he declared, were particularly suited for such purposes, and he proposed to give the Germans reprint rights to them for 2000 francs each.[35]

Both sides seemed satisfied with the meeting. Romberg considered Rubakin on the one hand an "idealist" and on the other "a shopkeeper."[36] In von Schubert's opinion Rubakin wanted first of all "to do business, to see money, and was ready to postpone the realization of his plans."[37] While Rubakin would obviously be difficult to deal with, Romberg thought that his cooperation would be invaluable for the Germans. On October 5, attempting to demonstrate his interest, Romberg offered Rubakin a typewriter, and on the 7th Rubakin responded that he had an opportunity to buy a good used one for just 275 francs—Romberg could just send him the money. When Rubakin delivered his proposed list of books for the camp libraries, he assured Romberg that through his contracts he could buy the works for a discount under the list price.[38]

To his dismay, Rubakin found that dealing with the Germans was not so simple a task as he had expected. To be sure, he had little trouble in winning funding from Romberg for his planned book on Russia; on November 8 he told Romberg that the book would be completed within six months of his beginning work and that it would appear simultaneously in four languages: Russian, German, French, and English. The book, he asserted, would expose the artificial nature of Russia's alliance with "democratic England" and with "republican France."[39] The Germans dealt in turn with Felix Valyi, editor of *Revue politique internationale,* on the question of publishing the work. Rubakin then requested an honorarium of 10,000 francs, but although negotiations dragged on into 1917, the book never appeared.[40]

Rubakin was also disappointed by the Germans' cool reaction both to his proposed libraries and to his proposal for the reprinting of his own books. The Auswartiges Amt's expert in the Russian language, Harald Cosack, refused several of Rubakin's writings on the grounds that they were either anti-German or pro-English. The Gemans eventually accepted five of the ten titles offered, paying Rubakin 10,000 francs as an honorarium, but he argued that they should have published his works as an integral collection.[41] The German critique of Rubakin's library plans called the level of the collection low and characterized the tone of the books as being generally neutralist and socialist. The proposed libraries, moreover, were weak in belles lettres, which the prisoners were most requesting.[42] Nevertheless Rubakin finally won German agreement for the establishment of three model camp libraries. On October 5, 1916, Rubakin formally notified Romberg that two of the collections had been shipped on September 21, the third on October 4. The letter, bearing the stamp of the Russian Mutual Aid Committee of Montreux, made no mention of Rubakin's private arrangements with Romberg and simply asked the ambassador to forward the books to Germany.[43]

Rubakin's model libraries, each containing over 600 titles, were composed of books published legally in Russia before 1914. They were aimed, he explained in a formal prospectus, at encouraging the "brotherhood and unity of peoples, since no war is eternal." They allegedly contained no Russian patriotism or chauvinism. Authors included were Belinsky, Dobroliubov, Herzen, Pisarev, Rubakin, Miliukov, Kliuchevsky, Kropotkin, Tugan-Baranovsky, and Tolstoy.[44]

Despite the large sums which he received from the Germans, Rubakin still maintained a free hand in his various maneuverings. When the Ford Peace Mission came to Switzerland in February 1916, Rubakin openly discussed his projects with Louis Lochner. According to Lochner, he admitted his contacts with the Germans: "I had figured correctly that the German authorities would be caught by my denunciation of the Tsar, and that on this score they would be glad to have the literature admitted, hoping that from their hatred of the Tsar, they would turn to a love of the Kaiser. That I was merely using the Tsar as a type, but that in reality my propaganda was directed against all exploitation of the many by the few—this the Geman military censors were too stupid to understand. My readers, however, understood. And when Russia's great moment comes, this propaganda work will bear fruit a hundredfold."[45] The German military censors, as noted, were not nearly so stupid as Rubakin claimed.

The Ford mission aroused great hopes in certain circles, even as it drew scorn and suspicion from Entente diplomats. An English officer spoke of it as "impregnated with intellectuality,"[46] and the French would not even permit the group to enter their country. Working with Biriukov and Henri Guilbeaux, a French radical then living in Geneva, Rubakin approached Lochner with a request for financial aid for his program of providing reading materials for prisoners of war. Lochner seemingly gave him some encouragement with the result that Rubakin tried to recruit other intellectuals to join him in making a formal application for funding. He failed in his immediate purpose, but he succeeded in making several contacts which eventually grew into lasting friendship.

The most notable of these new contacts was Romain Rolland, a French writer who had come out firmly against the war already in 1914. Through a Swiss friend, Prof. Auguste Forel, Rubakin met Rolland at the end of February 1916, but when Rubakin imprudently added Rolland's name to the commission of control for the project which he planned to submit to Lochner, Rolland protested vigorously. He objected to having his name used without his approval, and in any case he wanted no part of the "Ford millions." Rubakin apologized, and while he too never received any of the Ford millions, the relationship between the two writers eventually developed into a close friendship.[47]

In the spring of 1916 Rubakin launched a new career as a contributor to Swiss newspapers. The impetus for this came from Polish friends. In his work on the national question for the third volume of *Sredi knig,* he had established extensive contacts with Polish emigres in Switzerland, including Jan Kucharzewski, Simon Askenazy, and Bronislaw Pilsudski. He even came to speak with them of the possibility of obtaining a subsidy for a Polish version of his great book.

In the winter of 1915-1916, under Russian pressure, the French had banned discussion of the Polish question in the Parisian press. This edict struck directly at a French Swiss journalist, Edmond Privat, who had been publishing articles under several names in different newspapers. Silenced in Paris, Privat now returned to Switzerland where he could write freely.[48] With encouragement—and possibly funds—from the Poles, Rubakin decided to add his own voice to the rising discussion of the Polish question.[49]

Rubakin drafted his article first as a letter to the editor, but in translating it from Russian into French, he recast it as an article. His argument was that the Russian government was incapable of offering the Poles anything substantial in the way of national rights. When he submitted the piece to the *Gazette de Lausanne,* the newspaper's editor, Edouard Secretan, questioned, "Can't one dream of a more liberal Russia which will guarantee Poland an autonomy worthy of the name?" Rubakin responded by adding the thought that the fate of the Poles was bound "to the success of the Russian liberation movement," which, he predicted, was closer than most thought.[50]

The article caused a minor sensation in Switzerland, coming as it did from the pen of a well known Russian writer. Comment in the Swiss press continued for more than a month. Rubakin received letters of congratulations from such figures as Rolland, Forel, and Henryk Sienkiewicz, the Polish writer. Anatole Lunacharsky wrote, "The article will have a European resonance. But you yourself have made more than a few enemies! And, of course, friends!"[51]

Stimulated by this success, Rubakin submitted more articles to Swiss publications, but his views were out of tune with the Francophile and generally pro-Entente spirit of western Switzerland.[52] In a letter to the *Tribune de Lausanne,* he complained that a recently published article had been "completely devoid of facts," and he offered the newspaper one of his own works. "To give support to Russian reactionaires," he wrote, "is only to betray Russian democracy." The newspaper nevertheless rejected his argument and insisted on the necessity of an Allied victory over Germany.[53]

The *Gazette de Lausanne* rejected a proposed article on Germanophilism in the Tsarist government. "It seems to be inopportune," wrote Secretan, "to attack the Russian government at this moment." Rubakin replied that he was attacking the Tsarist regime only because "I am a Russian patriot; I love my people and my country." His views, Rubakin insisted, were "those of Russian progressive, non-revolutionary democracy." Secretan answered, "I believe that I see these things as you do. But still shouldn't one ask whether all truth should be uttered on every occasion, and whether one should not choose the moment?"[54]

The *Journal de Genève* raised similar objections to Rubakin's contributions. In rejecting a proposed article, George Wagniere wrote on January 1, 1917, "Among other things you speak of the government and of the Tsar in too aggressive a tone, which does not fit into our columns." Nevertheless on January 4 Wagniere accepted an article on Rasputin.[55]

When his articles were accepted, Rubakin's tendency to express himself at great length sometimes caused other problems. J. E. David, of the *Gazette de Lausanne,* complained on one occasion, "You have offered an article; I have accepted an article. But you send me a book." David had to cut the article into two sections for publication.[56]

In April 1917 Rubakin was able to write to Reichesberg, "Since May I have had to act as a local Swiss writer and to take upon myself the task of informing Europe about Russian affairs."[57] On the other hand, his journalistic efforts also brought trouble. In August 1916, V. M. Felkner of the Russian mission in Bern complained, "You have deprived me of any possibility of giving you these governmental materials when you publish articles with a content contradicting that which one can write abroad about one's own government in a time of struggle for Russian frontiers."[58] To this Rubakin responded that Felkner's letter had revealed that the boundaries between Russians were greater than those between Germans and Russians. He challenged Felkner to prove that he had written anything but the truth about

Russia. The Russian government was not identical with the Russian people, he concluded: "Please accept my sincere regret that even such good and honorable persons such as you are under the power of the position which they hold."[59]

By the time of the revolution in Russia in March of 1917, Rubakin had openly committed himself to the cause of revolution. In the past he had frequently insisted that he could still return to Russia; now, without a change of government, Rubakin could not hope to be permitted to return to his homeland.

V   THE REVOLUTIONS OF 1917

The collapse of Tsarist rule in Russia brought joy and exultation to the emigres in Switzerland. Reports of the Tsar's abdication reached them on March 15, 1917[1] and they immediately turned to congratulate each other and to discuss the possibilities of returning home. Bronislaw Pilsudski wrote to Rubakin, "I hasten to congratulate you and all your co-workers heartily on this event which is so great and beyond hopes."[2] Another Pole, Jan Perlowski, declared to Rubakin, "It is difficult to say anything at such a time. Long live the great free Russian people and all its sons who, like you, have struggled for freedom and have heralded it through difficult days."[3]

Rubakin wrote to Naum Reichesberg, "The past will not return. I am sure that in the very near future there will begin the sublimation and recrystallization of social relations everywhere."[4] Reichesberg responded in kind, writing, "I, dear Nikolai Alexandrovich, am seized by a passionate desire to return to Russia and to dedicate my humble powers to the service of Russian democracy."[5]

The emigres soon were dismayed to discover that the revolution in Russia would not, and probably could not, fulfill all their hopes. The Provisional Government, led by the liberals who were determined to continue the war effort, looked with disfavor on the return of those emigres who had clearly opposed the war effort. When Lenin and others chose to challenge the attitude of the government by returning through Germany, the government's inability to block them reflected poorly on its authority. Even after socialists in Petrograd had begun to enter the cabinet, the Provisional Government could not win the general support of the emigres.[6]

The contradictions of the February Revolution, as viewed from the emigration, were epitomized by the arrival in Switzerland, in the summer of 1917, of a special commission charged by the Provisional Government with investigating the activities of the Tsarist secret police, the Okhrana. The chief investigator in Switzerland, S. V. Svatikov, was an old friend of Rubakin, who wrote to him complaining about the activity of the Russian consul in Geneva, Leon Gornostaev.

Svatikov, in response, expressed regret that he could not get together with Rubakin to discuss books—"I have not read *one* book since February 27, that is revolution for you"—and went on to complain about the Russian diplomatic mission: "And what a cesspool our 'abroad' is, and especially Switzerland. All the servants of the old regime are at their posts."[7] As far as the emigres were concerned, the revolution had wrought few visible changes.

For Rubakin the revolution had the immediate effect of offering new journalistic opportunities. As he informed Reichesberg, "I have given up on the publication of my great book and have decided to publish it in parts."[8] These parts took the shape of articles and pamphlets. In a letter to a Ukrainian friend, Rubakin declared that his philosophy now was that which he had himself expressed in his work *Sredi knig:* "We will look above all at that which unites people and not at that which divides them."[9] He watched the succeeding stages of revolution in Russia with both fear and hope, uncertain as to his own future.

On March 19, George Wagniere, editor of the *Journal de Genève,* who had previously been so critical of Rubakin, requested two columns on the "leaders of the Russian revolution." Rubakin provided five, which were then divided into two articles. Rubakin saw the revolution as beginning a new era in world history, and he welcomed the accession to power of men whom he called his friends. He spoke of his long acquaintance with Miliukov, and he called the Kadet leader a "distinguished historian and sociologist," a "profoundly cultivated and Europeanized man."[10]

This effusive praise of Miliukov sounds curious in view of Rubakin's description, in a different context, of his conversations with Miliukov when the latter visited Switzerland in 1916. Writing in 1922, Rubakin declared that upon meeting after a separation of some ten years, he and Miliukov had found a deep rift between them, "the same one which separates all militarists from anti-militarists." Nevertheless he attributed Miliukov's failure in 1917 to the man's basic sincerity and honesty.[11]

In the spring of 1917 Rubakin was balancing as wide a variety of friendships and contacts as he had ever managed. Through his friendship with Miliukov, he had dealings with Victor Toporov, Miliukov's agent in Switzerland. He also maintained his friendship with Gregory Alexinsky, while he remained close to his pacifist friends such as Biriukov and Rolland. He even could deal with a wide variety of nationalists. He was close to Poles such as Perlowski and Pilsudski, but at the same time he could work with a Ukrainian such as Count Michael Tyszkiewicz, who complained bitterly of Polish imperialism.[12]

Because of his reputation, Rubakin drew still more people to him.

One example was George Herron, an American, who claimed to be the personal envoy of President Woodrow Wilson. When Herron became active in Switzerland in the fall of 1916, he immediately contacted Rubakin. (Since Herron, who called himself a Christian Socialist, advocated a war to the end against Germany, Prof. Adolphe Ferriere, who arranged for Rubakin to meet the American, suggested that it would be best if Biriukov, the pacifist, were not present.[13]) Herron's intention obviously was to impress Rubakin and presumably to obtain information of some sort. Inviting Rubakin to come to Geneva as his guest, he promised that the Russian could meet "three or four of my other important friends." In May he invited Rubakin to meet "a very important member of the British Foreign Office."[14]

In commenting on the revolution in Russia, Herron declared, "If it continues firmly on its way, with no break in its continuity, the revolution in Russia will be the greatest political initiative in the history of the world, greater even than the revolution in France." The Russian revolution, he continued, "will free the spirit of man in a way such as no German or Anglo-Saxon revolution would be capable of doing." Russia, however, must keep on its path "without compromise with either the reaction on the one side or anarchist impulses on the other." In conclusion, he asked Rubakin whether he ought to send Miliukov a copy of his book, *The Menace of Peace*.[15]

When Miliukov left office in May 1917, Rubakin, as might have been expected, found still more acquaintances in the government. As he wrote to the Belgian bibliographer Paul Otlet on May 25, "The socialists who have entered the new cabinet are good friends of mine. They are very serious types, solid and full of good practical sense."[16]

During the summer of 1917, Rubakin published several works critical of the Tsarist regime and extolling the revolution.[17] These received excellent reviews, and in August the *Gazette de Lausanne* named him a collaborator. Rubakin even offered his services to *Le Temps* in Paris, but without success. *Die Neue Zürcher Zeitung* also rejected his proposed articles, pleading a lack of space.[18]

As the revolution in Russia developed, however, Rubakin's views changed. In 1916 he had insisted that he was against "a peace at any price for my country."[19] By the summer of 1917 he was convinced Russia needed peace. Whereas the pro-Entente editors decried the growing movement toward peace in Russia and complained of political disintegration in the revolution, Rubakin chose to emphasize Russia's need for a quick end to the war despite the protestations of Britain and France to continue fighting. As a result, he began to have difficulty in placing his proposed articles, and he even found himself attacked in the French press. In October a Parisian journalist called for "an end to the spread of Rubakinist lamentations and other such pap."[20]

In rejecting one manuscript, Wagniere complained, "As for me, I remain convinced that the continuation of the present state of things will lead Russia not only to defeat and to anarchy but also to ruin and dismemberment." When Rubakin offered the *Journal de Genève* an article explaining why Russia needed peace, Wagniere exclaimed, "The consequences of the Russian Revolution are too sad for the cause of the Allies."[21]

Rubakin's Swiss friends frequently echoed these feelings. Prof. Adolphe Ferriere had protested in April, "You Russian pacifist socialists are preparing the downfall of Europe." In December he urged Rubakin to be more critical of the Germans in his writings.[22]

Rubakin expounded his views of the revolutionary year at length in a memorandum which he submitted to the French ambassador in Switzerland, M. Beau, on December 18, 1917, a month after the Bolshevik seizure of power in Petrograd. The Allies, he insisted, were at fault for their failure to recognize "their unequal forces from the military, economic, industrial, and financial point of view relative to the continuation of the war, and they have taken even less account of the difference in mentalities of peoples and of individuals."

Russia could not sustain a long war, Rubakin continued, while the Western Allies obviously had time on their side in the struggle with the Central Powers. Because of their failure to consider Russia's weakness, the Allies had erred grossly in their judgment of every Russian defeat as evidence of treason and in their view that the Bolsheviks were German agents.

Speaking in the name of "the true democracy" of Russia, Rubakin argued that Russia could not continue the war "in the present conditions of general fatigue and complete disorganization." To attempt to continue the war was "dangerous for the very cause of democratic and socialist revolution." Echoing a frequent cry of 1917, Rubakin warned, "Either the revolution will conquer the war or the war will conquer the revolution."

The Provisional Government in Russia, Rubakin explained, had failed to win the loyalty of the people because of its failure to work unswervingly for peace, its vacillation in the question of land reform, its refusal to consider the demands of the minority nationalities, and its delay in calling the Constituent Assembly. The Allies had to shoulder considerable blame for these failures because of their demonstrated hostility to the revolution: they had denied passports for the planned socialist conference in Stockholm, and they had openly sympathized with the counterrevolutionaries in Russia. The many Russian emigres who had not been able to return home, or who had returned only with difficulty, complained bitterly of the fact that British and French authorities had even taken control of Russia's frontiers.

In this situation, the Bolsheviks had emerged as the "true representatives of the Russian people, since their slogan is "Land and Peace." The Bolshevik seizure of power had been a "logical and almost inevitable fact." Lenin's party had come to power because its "precise program and above all its immediate execution corresponded to the views of the great majority of the Russian people." To regard the Bolsheviks as a "band" was to commit "the error of underestimating their forces." Regardless of any considerations about the tactics or the character of the Bolshevik party, Rubakin concluded, the basic program of the Bolsheviks was correct.[23]

Rubakin was also critical of Woodrow Wilson's Fourteen Points when these were issued in January 1918: "These amount to the old program of the Entente without the Russian demands," he charged. "Only Russian democracy defends the interests of all the people."[24]

Rubakin's outspoken views on the Bolshevik revolution aroused a strong reaction in French Switzerland. His voice quickly lost its authority and its audience. When he submitted an article entitled "La Russie reparatrice" to the Gazette de Lausanne, the editor rejected it with the comment that he saw the situation quite differently: "The Russian revolution, in effect, seems to us to have entered, unfortunately, onto a path anything but restored."[25]

Rubakin now found the outlets for political articles rapidly drying up, and he turned to biograp-hical sketches. It would seem that he preferred not to criticize the Bolshevik regime in print; the new Russian government included a number of old friends and acquaintances. The biographical sketches apparently offered a relatively non-controversial way to discuss the character of the Russian revolution.

His first sketch, published in March 1918, was of Lenin; Rubakin declared his own support of the revolution in Russia but expressed fears for its future under Lenin's direction.[26] Over the next few years, Rubakin wrote a number of other sketches of acquaintances, and in 1922 he compiled them in a large manuscript entitled "Great Figures of the Russian Revolution."[27] His choice of individuals and his attitude toward them clearly reflected his own interpretation of the revolutionary movement. Above all, he admired sincerity, dedication, and intellect; this combination led him to reckon among his friends persons totally antipathetic to each other: Breshko-Breshkovskaia, Vera Figner, Tolstoy, Miliukov, Plekhanov, Krupskaia, and Biriukov.

The sketches were of course very personal, and they fell far short of being comprehensive historical judgments of the individuals. They were to a great degree inconsistent as regards the criteria by which Rubakin measured each person but they embodied Rubakin's idea of his own role in the revolutionary movement as an educator rather than as a member of any one party. Much as he enjoyed his publistic work, Rubakin still found time for what he considered his more important studies of the reading public and also for his popular writing. In October 1916, with the aid of several Swiss intellectuals such as Ferriere and Prof. Auguste Forel, Rubakin opened a section on bibliopsychology within the institutional framework of the Rousseau Pedagogical Institute in Geneva. Rubakin served as director of the section, and in fact he was its only regular member. With this formal academic certification for his library, Rubakin continued his efforts to define the relationship between readers and books.[28]

His theories aroused no little opposition. By emphasizing the receptivity of the reader in his analysis of a book's impact, Rubakin seemed to some to be denying the book any objective value of its own. Romain Rolland felt constrained to "defend the book" against Rubakin's views: "When you say that bibliopsychology shows that 'what a book awakes in the soul of a reader depends on that soul and not on the book,' I think that the book too should be taken into account, since to recognize that the book is only a weapon is to recognize that it is not only a weapon, and it is not a matter of indifference whether a book is good or bad."[29] Another commentator compared Rubakin's theory with the idea that medicine had no innate value because of its varying effect on sick persons.[30]

Much of Rubakin's attention in 1917 was of course focused on the possible development of the Russian book market. Shortly after the February Revolution, Gulbinsky drew a dismal picture of conditions in Russia: "It is sad to see. Finally the people have achieved freedom of the press, and there is nothing to read. A tragedy. We need arrangements on a national scale. I have written to Manuilov [Minister of Education in the Provisional Government], but there is nothing to expect from him. We are engaged in publishing pennypinching." Gulbinsky complained that publishers were putting out editions of only tens of thousands when millions were needed: "The craving is incredible." Gulbinsky saw as the task of the day, "the greatest possible expansion of publishing activity."[31]

Publishers now found their stocks rapidly depleting as the reading public demanded more books; it was only now that the first two volumes of *Sredi knig* were sold out. In September Gulbinsky wrote of the difficulties in organizing typographic work, but he also had hopes for new projects. In particular he spoke of the need of a popular series "for the average village reader (you would do this masterfully)." It might be possible, Gulbinsky speculated, to begin the project by winter.[32]

The Bolshevik revolution intervened to alter the picture drastically. Local soviets throughout the country embarked on their own publishing programs without any concern for author's rights, and Rubakin could only watch in anguish as his works were widely republished while he received no royalties. According to the holdings of the Lenin Library in Moscow, there were at least 32 printings of various of Rubakin's works between 1917 and 1920.

Frustrated by the situation in Russia, Rubakin responded eagerly to prospects of other mass markets. When the American YMCA (Young Men's Christian Association) approached him with a proposal for the publication of a series of works for use among Russian prisoners of war and also Russian soldiers in France, he agreed with enthusiasm. At the same.time, he sought to reserve rights for these publications within Russia.

Rubakin's contact within the YMCA organization was a minister from New York City, Julius Hecker (in Russian: Gekker), who had received his Ph.D. from Columbia University with a dissertation on Russian sociology.[33] Hecker had hired Paul Biriukov as his aide in selecting Russian literature. In the summer of 1917 Rubakin quickly agreed to write a series of popular books on topics in the natural sciences—perpetual motion, chemistry, and astronomy.[34] Rubakin particularly welcomed the royalties, totalling 1500 francs in September and October 1917; he also revived his proposals for the establishment of a network of lending libraries within the prisoner of war camps.

The connection with the YMCA led Rubakin now to revive a topic on which he had wanted to write even before the war. He had long envisioned writing a philosophical, moralizing treatise on "The Great Words." When he had offered this idea to Ksenofont Tikhomirov in 1911, the publisher had rejected it, declaring that it would be immediately confiscated. "Every word," Tikhomirov exclaimed, "undermines the authority and the position of the Church."[35]

Rubakin's proposal aroused some uneasiness among officials of the YMCA. Conservative Russians who were close to these officials expressed shock upon learning of Rubakin's participation in the publishing endeavors of the organization. Hecker apparently had the authority to accept Rubakin's scientific works on his own responsibility, and in this regard there was no trouble. "There can be no tendentiousness in science," he explained to Rubakin, "and you write from purely scientific premises."[36] Manuscripts concerning ethical and religious topics, however, were not in his domain, and the final decision lay in the hands of a committee.

Hecker agreed with the "tendency" of Rubakin's proposed work, but he warned, "It will be necessary nevertheless to exclude all the biting remarks about the church and the Bible which sometimes slip in with you."[37] Rubakin immediately complained about Hecker's attempt at censorship, but he agreed to a suggestion to divide the work in two. The first volume would discuss truth, knowledge, science, and faith; the second, good, love, beauty, honor, and conscience. The premises of the work, Rubakin explained, were: faith was separate from knowledge; faith was not subject to reason; external church practice differed from faith; at the basis of society and government lay ethical, Christian, and extraconfessional principles; any sort of party platform was unconditionally excluded, also polemics; there would be no socialist or Marxist doctrine.[38]

Hecker, who showed great enthusiasm for all of Rubakin's projects, won approval for the manuscript. Nevertheless he did not hesitate to send sections of the work back and to urge Rubakin not to use the word "lie" in discussing problems of interpreting the Bible. He also suggested that Rubakin consider the word "gratitude," not just in the sense of gratitude to one's own generation but in addition "historical gratitude to past generations, the fruits of which we now enjoy."[39]

At the beginning of December 1917, Hecker delivered the manuscript to the Benteli publishing firm in Bumpliz, near Bern, which was one of the very few Swiss publishers with Russian type. To his dismay he learned that as of December 1, costs had so risen that publication of the work would cost twice as much as had been estimated. It would be necessary, he notified Rubakin, to cut the manuscript.[40] In contrast to his dealings with most other publishers, Rubakin was both punctual and extremely cooperative in working with Hecker.

Hecker in turn requested Rubakin to write an introduction for his own book, *Znanie i vera* (Knowledge and Belief). He suggested that Rubakin might say that he did not mean to undermine the authority of religion but rather of superstition, "going under the cloak of religion." He might also add that religion was "necessary for a happy and normal life." Such an introduction, Hecker urged, would serve as an advertisement for Rubakin's own work. Rubakin responded that he would rather write a lengthy critique, dealing with the "necessity and usefulness of religion as distinct from belonging to an established church."[41]

Rubakin deeply appreciated Hecker's aid. In December 1917 Romain Rolland singled out Rubakin as one of the few men he knew who could be happy in those days. Rubakin, he declared, was "imbued with the young forces awakening in his immense people." Just two months later, in February, Rolland spoke of Rubakin as having been on the verge of suicide, but he had found new strength in working with the YMCA. At the same time, Rolland confessed that he could not appreciate Rubakin's work: "He showed me his plan, as always full of confusion and in a terribly abstract tone. I cannot understand how such a man, so devoid of the gift to narrate and to translate his ideas into realistic stories, can command such a broad popular audience in his own land. One must think that the Russian people have a more abstract brain than ours."[42]

In March Hecker reported that he was recommending that Rubakin be put on his payroll at not less than 1,000 francs per month, and Rubakin responded with gratitude: "It is especially joyful for me that I again find a point of application for my abilities."[43]

The cooperation between the two men extended into 1919. In the course of his work, Hecker became more and more sympathetic to the Bolsheviks; in the summer of 1918, describing a meeting with Jan Berzin of the Soviet diplomatic mission in Switzerland, Hecker wrote, "In general there is nothing to fear from these people; they are only too happy to accommodate any good person."[44] Eventually Hecker became a Communist. Although he and Rubakin fell out somewhat in 1919, they remained friends for a number of years thereafter.[45]

In 1921, the American YMCA felt obliged to respond to criticisms of its publishing program in Switzerland at the end of the war, both because of Hecker's political conversion and because of Russian emigre criticisms of Rubakin's participation in the program. Noting that the program had been investigated by the State Department and the United States legation, the YMCA reaffirmed its faith in Rubakin's contributions: "The author formerly was a widely recognized atheistic materialist who came later in life to the philosophic Christian position. To the rationalist intellectuals of Russia, his present message appears constructive, regarded by them as a defense of faith rather than otherwise. At the same time the possibility of such writings disturbing others is frankly recognized." Rubakin's works, the YMCA insisted, may have lacked a clear religious character, but they could be recommended "from the ethical point of view."[46]

With the ending of his work for the YMCA, Rubakin faced the most difficult financial situation of his life. He had been unable to obtain any royalties for his publications in Soviet Russia, and most of his enterprises in Western Europe had now dried up. In the course of 1918, he had proposed, in cooperation with Biriukov, Rolland, and the Swiss theologian Leonhard Ragaz, the establishment of a pacifist institute, and he sought funds from German and American sources. He also spoke with Hecker about the possibility of giving the YMCA his library and also of bringing his Institute for Bibliopsychology within the framework of the association.[47] When all these ideas failed, he found himself extremely hardpressed, and at the same time he had to adjust both to the new Russian emigration and to the new order in Soviet Russia.

VI RUBAKIN AND SOVIET RUSSIA

At the time of the February Revolution in Russia, Rubakin had immediately entertained hopes of returning to his homeland. His passport, however, had expired, and he could obtain no aid from the Russian diplomatic mission in the summer of 1917. He suspected that Leon Gornostaev, the consul in Geneva who maintained an intelligence network in western Switzerland, had compiled a denunciatory dossier on him, and he vainly sought S. V. Svatikov's intervention on his behalf.

After the Bolshevik revolution, Rubakin, tied down by his large library and still lacking a passport, could only watch and wait. As he declared in his report to the French Ambassador, he viewed the Bolsheviks as embodying the will of the Russian people, especially in the question of continuing the war, but he did not support their party. The characterization of Lenin which he published in March 1918 made clear his fears about the course of the revolution.

Partly under the influence of his secretary, Mme. Schneeuhr, Rubakin was now becoming increasingly interested in the doctrines of Christian Science. (Romain Rolland urged him to investigate Bahaism, which Rolland considered more suitable "than American evangelism to the Russian popular spirit."[1]) Rubakin was also becoming ever more pacifist, and he was particularly distressed by the Red Terror in Russia in the late summer of 1918.

When the Swiss government accepted a Soviet diplomatic mission headed by Jan Berzin in May 1918, it essentially granted *de facto* recognition to the Soviet government.[2] Rubakin, who always felt that his fate was inextricably intertwined with Russia's, approached the mission with a new request for a passport and also with an inquiry about the possibility of his collecting royalties for the reprinting of his works by the Soviet government. At the same time, he listened hopefully to the views of his friend Biriukov, who obtained a passport from the mission and travelled to Soviet Russia in the fall, enthusiastic about the cultural work of the new regime.[3]

In the fall of 1918, as the war ended in Western Europe, social conflicts in Switzerland culminated in a general strike.[4] The Swiss government blamed the Soviet mission for much of the trouble and expelled it. The authorities, concerned about the activities of all the Russian emigres, went on to conduct an extensive investigation, deporting many persons whom they suspected of collusion with the Soviet representatives. Rubakin too fell prey to this "Bolschewiki-Untersuchung," as it came to be called, but searches produced no evidence against him.[5]

When the Swiss deported several Socialist Revolutionaries whom they considered supporters of the Soviet regime—the Left SR's had broken with the Bolsheviks in July—Rubakin attempted to rally the support of Swiss intellectuals on behalf of several of them. The liberal intellectuals responded, albeit in vain, but Rubakin continued to have the image in Switzerland of being pro-Bolshevik. When he made a brief trip to Czechoslovakia in 1919, he met with considerable difficulty in obtaining the right to return to Switzerland.[6]

In the early 1920s, the Swiss showed a disinclination to deal with the Soviet government, and the situation was seriously aggravated in 1923 when V. V. Vorovsky, a Soviet diplomat attending the Lausanne conference on the Eastern Question, was assassinated by a White Russian emigre of Swiss origin. A jury in Lausanne subsequently acquitted the assassin, and the Soviet government retaliated by refusing for several years to attend any meetings of international agencies held in Switzerland. In the absence of formal diplomatic relations, the representative of the Soviet Red Cross, Sergei Bagotsky, served as the unofficial representative of the Soviet government, while Rubakin's library came to serve as a sort of cultural representation.[7]

By 1920, when he moved from Baugy to Lausanne, Rubakin had apparently decided that he would remain in Switzerland, but he understood that the fate of his library and his life's work remained closely tied to Russia. Through Biriukov, who made annual trips to Moscow, he entreated Soviet officials for royalties and also for the new books now appearing in Russia. He briefly considered joining Biriukov in a venture to publish books for the Russian market.[8] Rubakin directed his appeals especially to his old friends in Moscow such as V. D. Bonch-Bruevich, Anatole Lunacharsky, and Nadezhda Krupskaia. Books began to come to him almost immediately, but several years passed before Gosizdat and other Soviet publishers began to send royalties.

Rubakin's unhappy position in 1921 and 1922 was exemplified by his correspondence with the writer Maxim Gorky. He wrote in November 1921 to request Gorky's assistance in publishing his works in Russia, and after long receiving no answer, he wrote again in January 1922, speaking this time of his desire "to do everything possible to keep his

N. A. Rubakin in his Lausanne library,
in the early 1940's.

N. A. Rubakin in Geneva. Sitting: N. Biriukor, N. Rubakin
Standing: on right, son A. N. Rubakin.

Maison Lambert in Bangy

library for Russia." Gorky responded that he had no connection with the Soviet publishing world and that he doubted whether the Soviet government had the money to purchase Rubakin's library. Rubakin immediately protested that he had not meant to sell his library; in fact he only wanted to assure that it would not have to be sold to pay his debts. Yet he still approached the Soviet government in the fall of 1922 with a proposal for the "nationalization" of his collection; the Soviet government did not agree.

Depressed, Rubakin again turned to Gorky with a lament on the unhappy plight of the intellectual: "All people are alone, but of all people the most alone is the writer. And the more gifted he is with talent and love for what is on the earth, i.e., for humanity, the more alone he is. And readers understand still less his thoughts, his feelings, his words, his intentions, and sufferings."

Gorky replied that he was somehow no longer used to receiving such letters: "Yes, we are all alone, more or less. This heavy solitude of the Russian intelligentsia among the Russian people has been long known to me, and it disturbed me even in the days of my youth. I have tried more than once to reflect this in my stories. But what can one say about this. Our game is played, our song sung, and not badly. Sometime," Gorky concluded, "wise people will be able to appreciate your diligent, enormous work of a true democrat. You have done much for the inspiration of the popular masses—I know this very well."[9]

Rubakin also hoped to obtain money from Soviet Russia to support his work in Switzerland. After publishing a study on bibliopsychology in French, he sent a copy to his old friend Viacheslav Karpinsky for his comments. Karpinsky was very critical of the work, complaining about both the translation and the printing. He considered the writing uneven—in some places clear and exact, in others, disconnected. Overall, he thought, the work lacked a clear plan. As for Rubakin's thesis that the quality of the book was secondary to the receptiveness of the reader, Karpinsky objected that if so, he had never read "a more pessimistic book than yours." The practical section of the work, he argued, contradicted the theoretical section, and Karpinsky complained that Rubakin would seem to have lost the clear class consciousness of his earlier years.

As for Rubakin's hopes for aid in his work, Karpinsky declared that he read such works with an eye to the use of the printed word as a weapon to aid propagandists and agitators. For this purpose he had found but little. Only Soviet Russia, Karpinsky concluded, could offer Rubakin the proper working conditions; its leaders understood that "the written and spoken word is what it really is: a weapon of class struggle." Rubakin should return to Russia to head such an institute.[10]

In the course of the 1920s, Rubakin gradually brought his financial situation into better order. The number of persons coming to use his library grew annually. Between 1913 and 1915, some 180 readers had borrowed books, and from 1915 to 1917 the figure had grown to 240. In 1925, on the other hand, the number of visitors totalled about 500; in 1931 this figure had grown to 1564; and in 1939 more than 1600 persons came to his library.[11]

In the 1920s the League of Nations turned to him for help in compiling bibliographies of Soviet publications. For a few years, he even compiled a bibliography on children's books for Soviet institutions. He also carried out a number of bibliographical projects for local Swiss organizations and institutions.

In 1929 Rubakin renamed his Institute of Bibliopsychology as the International Institute for Bibliographical Psychology, but the change of name represented no change in its structure. Rubakin and his secretary constituted the staff, while Rubakin received persons from all parts of the globe who wanted to study with him. These persons might stay for just a week or two or perhaps for considerably longer.

Rubakin still had many grand plans for publications, but somehow only his work on bibliopsychology could find the way into print. He negotiated with Russian publishers in the west on his "Tragediia russkogo naroda," and he entertained dreams of a massive third edition of *Sredi knig*, this time to be an encyclopedia of books, but these plans fell through.[12]

His old works still remained popular in the 1920. A study of the use of books in a Moscow lending library which served workers in factories found that in 1923 and 1924 there was a greater demand for Rubakin's books on nature an and geography than there was for any other nonfiction works: "Both the old and the young, both men and women read Rubakin. He has an especially great influence on the poorly developed, beginning readers; they read some of his books through several times."[13] His works had a similar popularity within Russian emigre colonies in the west.

In 1930 Rubakin's financial position was significantly improved when the Soviet government agreed to grant him a pension.[14] In 1934 he wrote to a friend, "In July I will be 72 years old. . . You ask how I am living. I have been here working in Switzerland for 25 years now, never for a minute feeling cut off from my native land."[15]

New currents, however, were already flowing through Russia. Writing in 1932, A. Rubinshtein accused Rubakin of having been one of the bourgeois theoreticians who had been allegedly holding Soviet bibliography prisoner and presumably hindering it from meeting the tasks of the day. Claiming that Rubakin had failed to distinguish the role of the book in Soviet society as opposed to its role in capitalist society, Rubinshtein included him among the hostile writers, ranging from "popist idealist" to "Trotskyite Menshevik contraband," from whom Soviet writers had to free themselves.[16]

In 1935, the Soviet minister to Prague, A. Ya. Arosev, urged Rubakin to return to Soviet Russia, but as Rubakin's son has noted, "Many friends ceased to write to him. Others put him off with obscure phrases in answer to his questions as to why they did not publish him. Rubakin in no way could understand what was happening."[17]

Rubakin was now cut off from the Soviet Union. The Stalinist purges and the resulting tensions among the intellectuals in the USSR made contacts with emigres such as Rubakin appear dangerous and suspicious. The Soviet government continued his pension, but intellectually he had lost contact with his country. Even his once prolific pen fell silent.

His last major publication was an essay on bibliopsychology, written in conjunction with his assistant Maria Betmann.[18] Published in Paris in 1937, this effort summarized his years of work on the topic. Every book, he argued, provides the reader with "secondary engrams," vicarious experiences, and it contributes to building new combinations of existing engrams. Most librarians, he declared, "recommend a book for what they consider to be its content, disregarding the fact that in the reader's mnema [the total of accumulated engrams] it may produce a different reaction from their own." To understand a reader, the librarian must investigate and classify him or her according to biological, anthropological, social, and especially psychological criteria.

Readers may be divided in any number of ways: introvert or extrovert; pessimistic, optimistic, or aggressive; mystic or rationalist; given to inductive or deductive reasoning; interested in historical and evolutionary developments or concerned with "the coexistence of phenomena and their distribution in space."

Having analyzed the reader, the librarian should select the book best suited for that reader's wants, needs, and psychological type. In so doing, the librarian should work to raise the reader's cultural level. While not indulging in any form of censorship, the librarian must be acutely aware of the "potential" of the available books and have them suitably catalogued. To perform this task competently, the librarian himself must have synthetic, intuitive, extroverted, altruistic, and optimistic characteristics.

It was as a librarian that Rubakin was best known in the last decade of his life. His collection of books represented the major source in western Europe for information about Russia. Students, journalists, private individuals, institutions, and libraries all turned to him for materials and references. Although Rubakin had some trouble with the concern of Swiss authorities about the dissemination of "Communist propaganda," his library occupied an important place in Swiss intellectual life.

The Second World War brought him a new reading public, and his clientele grew rapidly. As he had over a quarter of a century earlier, he found he could serve the cultural needs of Russian prisoners of war in Germany. There were also many Soviet civilians and escaped prisoners of war interned in Switzerland. His son has estimated that about 10,000 such persons turned to Rubakin for aid.

Rubakin had no financial resources with which he could help these people, but he lent books, many of which he never received back. He also helped with problems of communications with Swiss authorities. This latter task was especially important because Switzerland and the Soviet Union still had no formal diplomatic relations. Within his resources, Rubakin served his native land willingly and unstintingly.

When the USSR and Switzerland finally reestablished relations after the war, Rubakin hoped to renew his ties with his homeland, but his health was bad. In the night of November 22-23, 1946, he died in his sleep at the age of 84. His body was cremated, and in 1948 the urn with his ashes was shipped to Moscow to be interred in the wall of the Novodevichii cemetery.

Confusion surrounded the disposition of his library. Rubakin had discussed the sale of his books with representatives of a number of institutions, including several major American universities. The Swiss National Library also expressed interest in the collection, but the Soviet government insisted that Rubakin had willed his library to the Soviet Union as part of the agreement concerning his pension. In 1948 the books were shipped to Moscow and incorporated into the Lenin Library under the signature "Rb." The loss of the collection, which has been variously estimated at from 75,000 to over 100,000 volumes, was a serious blow to western scholars and readers who had come to rely upon it.

The situation in regard to Rubakin's papers was infinitely more complicated. The Soviet government could press no legal claim to the papers, which now passed into the custody of his colleague Maria Betmann. The Soviet Union apparently agreed to continue to pay her the pension which it had been giving Rubakin, and she sold some two-thirds of Rubakin's papers to the Lenin Library. After her death in 1964 it was learned that the rest of the papers had been destroyed.[18]

EPILOGUE

Rubakin's career passed through a number of phases. During his years in St. Petersburg, he was probably best known for his popular works on scientific and historical topics, but he earned wide recognition at the same time for his efforts in promoting self-education among the masses and for his studies of the Russian reading public. After he went into the emigration, Rubakin won a different kind of fame with the publication of the second edition of *Sredi knig*, the first annotated recommendatory bibliography in Russian. His library served as a major Russian cultural center in Western Europe, and through his publications and his personal contacts, he contributed to the education of western intellectuals about Russia.

He was not so much a creative and original writer as a craftsman of words, an expert popularizer, and a master of bibliography. His popular works were not widely read by the intellectuals of Russia; they appealed far more to the developing reading public which needed materials which it could understand. For this Rubakin had a particular talent, and while few of his works are now worth reprinting, he understood and served his public well.

The intellectuals appreciated *Sredi knig* far more. The records of Rubakin's library show that many leading revolutionaries borrowed this work, and Rubakin must have drawn great satisfaction from such communications as the one he received from Vladimir Burtsev, who, having been exiled by the Tsarist government in 1915, reported that he had carried a copy of *Sredi knig* with him to Siberia.[1]

However great the volume of his publications, Rubakin's greatest achievements were probably not to be measured in terms of titles or pages. Rather they were reflected in the enormous correspondence which he carried on with readers and in the testimonies offered later by individuals speaking of his influence on them. These persons included workers and peasants as well as intellectuals. Rubakin had the power to inspire readers to continue to study. In this goal he was eminently successful.

Rubakin's role in the Russian revolutionary movement was largely one again of education. His own participation was limited, even when one considers his relationship with Azef. On the other hand, he deeply affected the intellectual development of the revolutionaries, their choice of reading materials, and he maintained a remarkable number of friends in the various political parties.

His capacity for understanding and communicating with persons of opposing political views was nowhere better illustrated than in his work with representatives of the various minority nationalities of Russia. His long essay on the national question in the truncated third volume of *Sredi knig* vividly demonstrated his sensitivity in comprehending the arguments of these intellectuals, and the essay is still valuable for students of the national question in Tsarist Russia.[2]

Rubakin's own conversion to Tolstoyan views was a long gradual process. His son has ascribed a great deal of influence in this regard to Rubakin's second wife and to his secretaries. Rubakin, however, had already demonstrated his sympathy for Tolstoy in the first volume of *Sredi knig*. His own acquaintance with Tolstoy, together with his friendship with Paul Biriukov and Romain Rolland, undoubtedly were at least as important as the influence of the women around him. One can also believe that the sunny, warm climate of the Lake of Geneva had an effect on him, and not to be underestimated is the fact that Rubakin was one of the persons to whom Tolstoy had addressed his statement on the "nonresistance to evil" in 1896. To have played such a historic role must have had a strong influence on Rubakin's thoughts.

After the Bolshevik revolution, Rubakin could not approve of the new order in Soviet Russia, but neither would he break with it completely. Despite occasional invitations to return, he remained an emigre. Nevertheless he realized his need to remain in direct contact with Russian books, and he maintained his personal ties with the Soviet intelligentsia as long as he could.

The ambiguity of Rubakin's life as a Russian in the emigration was symbolized by the lives of his children. His two sons by his second marriage remained in Switzerland and never took Soviet citizenship. His eldest son, Alexander Nikolaevich, after living in France, settled in the Soviet Union after the Second World War and took a leading role in the 1960s in the rebirth of interest in his father's work. Rubakin's second son, Michael, was reported missing as a Russian soldier during the First World War.

Rubakin's career illustrates the fact that party lines in Russia were more fluid before 1917, and probably even in Soviet Russia before Stalin's time, than many historical writings would lead us to believe. Rubakin, who wanted to emphasize "the things which bring men together," thought he could see the common goals of all the revolutionaries.

NOTES

I: INTRODUCTION

1. A. N. Rubakin, *Rubakin* (*Lotsman knizhnogo moria*)(Moscow, 1967), p. 63.

2. Gosudarstvennaia Biblioteka imeni Lenina (GBL), Otdel rukopisei (OR), Fond 358 (N. A. Rubakin), kart. 346, ed. khr. 2. See also Rubakin, *Rubakin,* pp. 5-7.

3. Rubakin, *Rubakin,* p. 97.

4. Cf. the comments in J. H. L. Keep, "1917: The Tyranny of Paris over Petrograd," *Soviet Studies,* 20: 24-26.

5. Rubakin has been the subject of three books published in the Soviet Union: A. N. Rubakin, *Rubakin;* L. V. Razgon, *Pod shifrom "Rb"* (Moscow, 1966); and K. G. Mavricheva, *N. A. Rubakin* (Moscow, 1972). On his bibliographical work, see also M. V. Mashkova, *Istoriia russkoi bibliografii nachala XX veka* (*do oktiabria 1917 goda*) (Moscow, 1969), pp. 184-209.

6. I was myself guilty of this in my *Russian Revolution in Switzerland, 1914-1917* (Madison, 1971). Cf. the assertion that he was the brother of either Naum or Julian Reichesberg in Stefan T. Possony, *Lenin: Compulsive Revolutionary* (Chicago, 1964), p. 189, and in Leonhard Haas, ed., *Lenin: Unbekannte Briefe 1912-1914* (Zurich, 1967), pp. 85-86.

7. See N. A. Rubakin, *Sredi knig,* 3 vols. (reprinted by Oriental Research Partners, Cambridge, England, 1973 with a new introduction by Alfred Erich Senn), 1: iii.

8. A. N. Rubakin, *Rubakin,* p. 10.

9. Ibid., p. 14.

10. A bibliography of Rubakin's works appears in GBL, *Zapiski otdela rukopisei,* 26: 152-206. See also the bibliography in Mavricheva, *N. A. Rubakin,* pp. 161-176.

11. A. N. Rubakin, *Rubakin,* p. 11.

12. Cf. N. A. Rubakin, *Sredi knig,* I: 236-237.

13. See his autobiographical note in *Bibliograficheskii sbornik*, vol. I, vyp. 2 (Petrograd, 1915), pp. 28-31 (76-79); also his autobiographical statement to the Soviet government in support of his petition for a pension, GBL, F. 358, 350/4.

14. "Velikie figury russkoi revoliutsii," MS in GBL, F. 358, 159/1-5.

15. Ibid., GBL, F. 358, 159/5.

16. See Alfred Erich Senn, "P. I. Biriukov: A Tolstoyan in War, Revolution, and Peace," *The Russian Review*, 32: 280.

17. GBL, F. 358, 159/5.

18. Ibid.

19. Ibid.

20. A. N. Rubakin, *Rubakin*, p. 18.

21. Autobiographical sketch in GBL, F. 358, 346/2.

22. N. A. Rubakin, "Opty programmy dlia issledovaniia literatury dlia naroda," *Russkoe bogatstvo*, 1889, no. 5-6, pp. 286-313.

23. GBL, F. 358, 346/2.

24. GBL, F. 358, 350/4; see also Mavricheva, *N. A. Rubakin*, p. 22.

25. *Rasskazy o velikikh i groznikh yavleniiakh prirody* (St. Petersburg, 1892), was republished in nine editions before the First World War and issued again by the Soviet government in 1929. It was translated into Armenian, Bulgarian, Buriat, Georgian, Yiddish, Kazakh, Latvian, Tatar, and Finnish. *Rasskazy o delakh v tsarstve zhivotnykh* (St. Petersburg, 1893), was republished in seven editions before the war and issued again by the Central Executive Committee in 1919. It was translated into Bulgarian, Georgian, Yiddish, Latvian, Lithuanian, and Udmurt.

26. See Mavricheva, *N. A. Rubakin*, p. 26.

27. GBL, F. 358, 159/5.

28. See Mavricheva, *N. A. Rubakin*, pp. 22-26.

29. A.N. Rubakin, *Rubakin*, p. 22.

II. THE PETERSBURG YEARS

1. See E. P. Aref'eva, "N. A. Rubakin—kak knigosobiratel' i ego biblioteki v Sovetskom Soiuze," *Kniga: Issledovaniia i materialy*, 8: 380-385.

2. Ibid., p. 385.

3. N. A. Rubakin, "Osnovnye zadachi bibliotechnogo dela," *Russkaia shkola*, 1907, no. 7-8, pp. 174-203.

4. A. N. Rubakin, *Rubakin*, p. 68.

5. See K. M. Derunov, *Primernyi bibliotechnyi katalog* (St. Petersburg, 1908-1911), pp. 153-158.

6. Aref'eva, "N. A. Rubakin," *Kniga*, 8: 383.

7. I. D. Sytin, *Zhizn' dlia knig* (Moscow, 1960), p. 138.

8. Cf. Lenin's citations of Rubakin in his *Polnoe sobranie sochinenii* (hereinafter referred to as *PSS*), 5th ed., 55 vol. (Moscow, 1960-1964), 16: 212, 17: 63, 23: 258-259.

9. Mavricheva, *N. A. Rubakin*, pp. 136-137.

10. A. N. Rubakin, *Rubakin*, pp. 35-36.

11. GBL, F. 358, 159/5.

12. N. A. Rubakin, *Pered rassvetom* (St. Petersburg, 1912), p. 8.

13. Ibid., pp. 13-27.

14. M. Gor'kii, *Sobranie sochinenii*, 30 vol. (Moscow, 1949-1953), 23: 325-327.

15. N. A. Rubakin, *Pered rassvetom*, pp. 79-91.

16. Ibid., p. 6.

17. Lev Tolstoi, *Polnoe sobranie sochinenii*, 90 vol. (Moscow, 1928-1958), 69: 127-140; P. I. Biriukov, *L. N. Tolstoi. Biografiia*, 3 vol. (Berlin, 1921), 3: 470-473.

18. GBL, F. 358, 159/5.

19. A. N. Rubakin, *Rubakin*, pp. 49-50.

20. GBL, F. 358, 159/5.

21. See GBL, F. 358, 159/3; A. N. Rubakin, *Nad rekoiu vremeni* (Moscow, 1966), pp. 28-29; V. Burtsev, *V pogone za provokatorami* (Moscow, 1928), pp. 108, 134.

22. N. A. Rubakin, *Pered rassvetom*, p. 237.

23. A. N. Rubakin, *Rubakin*, pp. 53-54.

24. GBL, F. 358, 346/1.

25. It is not clear how he obtained a legal passport, which he apparently needed in order to export his books. On conditions of emigration at this time, see Yu. F. Filipov, *Emigratsiia* (St. Petersburg, 1906).

III. IN THE EMIGRATION

1. See Senn, *The Russian Revolution*, pp. 5-7.

2. Ibid., pp. 7-8, 11.

3. M. Bronskii, "Uchastie Lenina v shveitsarskom rabochem dvizhenii," *Proletarskaia revoliutsiia*, 1924, no. 4, p. 39.

4. V. M. Velichkina, *Shveitsariia* (Moscow, 1918), p. 240. Velichkina was the wife of V. D. Bonch-Bruevich.

5. A. N. Rubakin, *Nad rekoiu uremeni*, p. 61.

6. See A. N. Rubakin, *Rubakin*, pp. 61-62.

7. Aref'eva, "N. A. Rubakin," *Kniga*, 8: 385-389.

8. GBL, F. 358, 245/23. On the Kuklin library, see V. D. Bonch-Bruevich, "Biblioteka i arkhiv RSDRP v Zheneve," *Krasnaia letopis'*, 1931, no. 3, pp. 106-134.

9. GBL, F. 358, 157/14.

10. On "Zemlia i volia," see Franco Venturi, *Roots of Revolution* (New York, 1966), pp. 558-632.

11. A. N. Rubakin, *Rubakin*, pp. 98-99.

12. The Bolsheviks lived in the Maison Vincent which lay just across the road from the Maison Lambert where Rubakin lived.

13. A. N. Rubakin, *Rubakin*, pp. 99-100.

14. See Samuel H. Baron, *Plekhanov: The Father of Russian Marxism* (Stanford, 1963), pp. 295-307.

15. GBL, F. 358, 159/5.

16. GBL, F. 358, 263/31.

17. Letter of September 11, 1909, GBL, F. 358, 263/28.

18. Plekhanov's letters, undated, GBL, F. 358, 263/30, and undated and July 14, 1915, GBL, F. 358, 263/31.

19. N. A. Rubakin, "N. Lenin-Uljanow als Mensch und Revolutionar," *Internationale Rundschau*, no. 4, March 15, 1918, pp. 87-105. On Rubakin's attitude toward Lenin, see also A. N. Rubakin, *Nad rekoiu vremeni*, pp. 60-62.

20. Burtsev, *V pogone za provokatorami*, p. 108.

21. GBL, F. 358, 159/5.

22. GBL, F. 358, 346/2.

23. M. V. D. to Zagranichnaia Agentura, May 31, 1910, Okhrana archive, Hoover Institution, Stanford, XIIIc (1), 1910; Zagranichnaia Agentura to M. V. D., June 17/30, 1910, Okhrana archive, XIIIb (1), 1910. The double-dating of the second document reflects the difference between the Gregorian calendar used in the West and the Julian calendar then still in use in Russia (until 1918).

24. A. N. Rubakin, *Nad rekoiu vremeni*, p. 68.

25. GBL, F. 358, 232/26.

26. GBL, F. 358, 234/14.

27. GBL, F. 358, 234/18.

28. GBL, F. 358, 233/20 and 234/18.

29. GBL, F. 358, 235/9.

30. Rubakin to Pozdeev, December 7, 1909, GBL, F. 358, 173/19.

31. Rubakin to Pozdeev, February 13, 1910, GBL, F. 358, 173/19.

32. On Gulbinsky-Vladislavev, see Mashkova, *Istoriia russkoi bibliografii*, pp. 214-218.

33. For a detailed account of the publication of *Sredi knig*, see Alfred Erich Senn, "The Publication of *Sredi knig*," introduction to N. A. Rubakin, *Sredi knig*, 1: V-XXVIII.

34. Ibid., p. XI.

35. Correspondence in GBL, F. 358, 234/18.

36. Letter of December 2, 1911, GBL, F. 358, 174/14. Cf. Rubakin's description of himself upon meeting Romain Rolland in 1916, in Romain Rolland, *Journal des années de guerre 1914-1919* (Paris, 1952), p. 699.

37. *Shkol'naia podgotovka vtoroi russkoi revoliutsii*, 4th ed. (St. Petersburg, 1913), pp. 197, 205.

38. *Priamyi put'*, V (May 1911), p. 153.

39. GBL, F. 358, 174/14.

40. Letter of December 14, 1911, GBL, F. 358, 263/29.

41. Correspondence in GBL, F. 358, 234/18.

42. GBL, F. 358, 233/22.

43. Letter of April 30, 1912, GBL, F. 358, 234/18.

44. Letter of July 4, 1912, GBL, F. 358, 235/10.

45. Letter of July 12, 1912, GBL, F. 358, 174/13.

46. GBL, F. 358, 233/22.

47. Correspondence in GBL, F. 358, 234/18-19.

48. GBL, F. 358, 233/22.

49. Letter of February 11, 1913, GBL, F. 358, 233/22.

50. Correspondence in GBL, F. 358, 174/14.

51. GBL, F. 358, 215/2, 168/46.

52. Lenin, *PSS*, 25: 111-114. See also M. A. Briskman, "Retsenziia V. I. Lenina na trud N. A. Rubakina i ee metodologicheskoe znachenie," *Trudy (Leningradskii gos. institut kul'tury im. N. K. Krupskoi)*, 22: 242-255.

53. L. M. Ivanova, A. B. Sidorova, and M. V. Charushnikova, "Arkhiv N. A. Rubakina," in GBL, *Zapiski otdela rukopisei*, 26: 117-123.

54. Cf. A. N. Rubakin, *Rubakin*, p. 118. On Rubakin's temper, cf. Romain Rolland's letter to Adolphe Ferriere, December 11, 1932, in Pierre Abraham, ed., *Romain Rolland* (Neuchatel, 1969), pp. 202-203.

IV. WORLD WAR I

1. See Senn, *The Russian Revolution*, pp. 15-29.

2. "Otchet o deiatel'nosti Imperatorskoi Missii v Shveitsarii," *Izvestiia Ministerstva Inostrannykh Del*, 4: 174-176.

3. Archive of the League of Swiss Relief Societies for Political Prisoners and Exiles of Russia, International Institute of Social History, Amsterdam.

4. Ibid.

5. Letter of October 15, 1914, GBL, F. 358, 266/48.

6. GBL, F. 358, 342/1.

7. See Lenin, *PSS*, 49: 405-406.

8. Letter of October 1, 1914, GBL, F. 358, 283/6.

9. GBL, F. 358, 266/48.

10. Letter of October 13, 1914, GBL, F. 358, 208/16.

11. See GBL, F. 358, 157/13; A. S. Kudriavtsev et al., *Lenin v Berne i Tsiurikhe* (Moscow, 1972), p. 105; *Vladimir Il'ich Lenin. Biograficheskaia khronika*, 4 vol. (Moscow, 1970-1973), 3:291; Okhrana report, no. 1698, November 13/26, 1914, Okhrana archive, XIIIb (1).

12. Letters of February 14 and July 14, 1915, GBL, F. 358, 263/31.

13. Correspondence in GBL, F. 358, 199/19.

14. GBL, F. 358, 282/47.

15. A. N. Rubakin, *Rubakin*, p. 101; Alfred Erich Senn, "Nikolai Rubakin's Library for Revolutionaires," *Slavic Review*, 32: 558.

16. GBL, F. 358, 157/13.

17. See Senn, "Nikolai Rubakin's Library." 554-559.

18. See Alfred Erich Senn, "The Politics of *Golos* and *Nashe Slovo*," *International Review of Social History*, 17: 675-704; Manuilsky's letter, GBL, F. 358, 252/36.

19. Correspondence in GBL, F. 358, 242/34.

20. See the correspondence with Artur Zifel'dt, GBL, F. 358, 230/41.

21. Senn, *The Russian Revolution*, pp. 167-175.

22. See Senn, "The Publication of *Sredi knig*," in N. A. Rubakin, *Sredi knig*, 1: XXII.

23. GBL, F. 358, 141/1.

24. Cf. his *Rossiia v tsifrakh*, 2nd ed. (St. Petersburg, 1912).

25. Ivanova et al., "Arkhiv N. A. Rubakina," GBL, *Zapiski otdela rukopisei*, 26: 86-87.

26. Romberg to Berlin, June 15, 1915, Auswärtiges Amt, Bonn (hereinafter referred to as AA), microfilm series T120, reel 4818/frame L244208. See also Gagern to Vienna, June 26, 1915, Haus-, Hof-, und Staatsarchiv, Vienna, PA, XXVII, 53/Berichte, 76.

27. Okhrana report no. 1697, December 13/26, 1914, Okhrana archive, XIIIb (1), 1914.

28. Protocol of the meeting in the papers of Isaac Bisk, Nicolaevsky collection, Hoover Institution, Stanford.

29. See K. M. Oberuchev, *V dni revoliutsii* (New York, 1919), pp. 8-15; summary of his activities in Okhrana report no. 153, February 13/26, 1916, Okhrana archive, XIIIb (1), 1916; Oberuchev's letter to Rubakin, November 17 [1918], GBL, F. 358, 259/10.

30. GBL, F. 358, 266/48.

31. AA, microfilm T120, 5224/K489037, K489043. See also Jerry H. Hoffman, "V. Stepankovsky, Ukrainian Nationalist and German Agent," *Slavonic and East European Review*, 50: 594-602.

32. AA, microfilm T120, 5224/K489037.

33. Ibid., 5224/K489189, K489233.

34. GBL, F. 358, 294/12.

35. AA, microfilm T120, 5224/K489194.

36. Ibid., 4818/L244001.

37. Memorandum of October 2, 1915, AA, Politisches Archiv, Ges. Bern, Sonderhefte über Personen, Bd. II. This file was microfilmed very incompletely.

38. AA, microfilm T120, 4818/L244001.

39. By February 1917, Romberg had paid some 20,000 francs in support of the project. See AA, Politisches Archiv. Ges. Bern., Sonderhefte, Bd. II.

40. Correspondence with Valyi, GBL, F. 358, 196/27, 325/6.

41. See Senn, *The Russian Revolution*, p. 140.

42. AA, Politisches Archiv, Ges. Bern, Sonderhefte, Bd. II.

43. AA, microfilm T120, 4818/L244039; GBL, F. 358, 191/21.

44. "Primernyi katalog knig dlia bibliotek dlia russkikh voennoplennykh," GBL, F. 358, 69/13.

45. Louis P. Lochner, "Henry Ford and His Peace Venture," Louis Lochner Papers, Wisconsin State Historical Society, Box 53.

46. Report by Commander W. L. Down, RN, Public Records Office, London, F.O. 371, 2803/3207.

47. See Forel's letter of February 29, 1916, GBL, F. 358, 303/1; Rolland's description of the meeting in his *Journal*, p. 699; the correspondence between Rolland and Rubakin, in GBL, *Zapiski otdela rukopisei*, 25: 432-463; A. N. Rubakin, *Rubakin*, pp. 106-112.

48. On Privat's activity, see "Edmond Privat, 1889-1962," *Revue neuchâteloise*, no. 43/44, pp. 28-39; the newspaper archive of the Centralna Agencja Polska w Lozannie, pudlo 230, Archiwum Akt Nowych, Warsaw, Poland.

49. S. Zielinski to M. Sokolnicki, letter of July 6, 1916, Pilsudski Institute, New York City.

50. *Gazette de Lausanne*, May 9, 1916. See also Alfred Erich Senn,

"A Russian Voice on the Polish Question, 1916," *The Polish Review*, vol. 19, no. 2, pp. 83-88.

51. GBL, F. 358, 249/33.

52. See his "La Reaction russe et son evolution," *Revue politique internationale*, 1916, no. 21, pp. 209-235, no. 22, pp. 28-55; "La Russie qui s'en va et la Russie qui vient," *Bibliothèque universelle et revue suisse*, 1916, no. 251, pp. 282-98, no. 252, pp. 474-492, and also printed separately (Lausanne, 1916).

53. Rubakin's letter of January 27, 1917, and the *Tribune's* response, January 29, 1917, GBL, F. 358, 325/20.

54. Correspondence in GBL, F. 358, 324/24 and 197/39.

55. GBL, F. 358, 324/32. In 1918 Wagniere served as the Swiss envoy in Italy.

56. "Lettres d'un russe sur la Russie," *Gazette de Lausanne*, January 23 and 25, 1917; GBL, F. 358, 324/24.

57. Letter of April 2, 1917, GBL, F. 358, 183/5.

58. GBL, F. 358, 282/47.

59. Letter of August 18, 1916, GBL, F. 358, 186/30.

V.: THE REVOLUTIONS OF 1917

1. The revolution took place in February according to the Julian calendar still in Russia and therefore it is referred to as the February Revolution, although in the West it was in March according to the Gregorian calendar.

2. GBL, F. 358, 263/4.

3. GBL, F. 358, 262/21.

4. Letter of April 2, 1917, GBL, F. 358, 183/5.

5. Letter of May 5, 1917, GBL, F. 358, 266/48.

6. On Lenin's return see Alfred Erich Senn, "New Documents on Lenin's Departure from Switzerland, 1917," *International Review of Social History*, 19: 245-276. St. Petersburg was renamed "Petrograd" in 1914.

7. Correspondence in GBL, F. 358, 184/20 and 273/24. The results of the investigation were published in V. A. Agafonov, *Zagranichnaia okhranka* (Petrograd, 1918); *Recueil de documents secrèts tirés des archives de l'ancien Ministère des Affaires Etrangères Russe* (Geneva, 1917).

8. GBL, F. 358, 183/5.

9. Letter to Michael Tyszkiewicz, March 30, 1917, GBL, F. 358, 280/61; N. A. Rubakin, *Sredi knig*, 1: 191.

10. "Les chefs de la revolution russe," *Journal de Genève*, March 24 and 25, 1917; GBL, F. 358, 324/32.

11. GBL, F. 358, 159/5.

12. Tyszkiewicz to Rubakin, October 20, 1915, GBL, F. 358, 280/60.

13. Letter of October 22, 1916, GBL, F. 358, 301/29.

14. Correspondence in GBL, F. 358, 305/19.

15. Letter of April 7, 1917, GBL, F. 358, 305/19. On Herron's activity among the Russians in Switzerland, see Mitchell Pirie Briggs, *George D. Herron and the European Settlement* (Stanford, 1932), pp. 135-149. Herron's *The Menace of Peace* was published in both London and New York at the beginning of 1917.

16. GBL, F. 358, 195/9.

17. He published articles in *Internationale Rundschau, Journal de Genève, Die Freie Zeitung, Die Weissen Blätter,* and *Gazette de Lausanne,* in addition to his *Qu'est-ce que la revolution russe* (Geneva, 1917).

18. Letter from Abram Charasch, October 9, 1917, GBL, F. 358, 284/39.

19. In a letter of May 24, 1916, to Paul Otlet, he also denied that he was a Tolstoyan. GBL, F. 358, 195/9.

20. Pierre Giffard, "La Censure pour tous," *L'Auto,* October 24, 1917.

21. Letters of October 8 and 29, 1917, GBL, F. 358, 324/32.

22. GBL, F. 358, 301/29.

23. GBL, F. 358, 133/1.

24. Undated telegram to Beek den Donk de Jong, GBL, F. 358, 194/2.

25. Letter of February 1, 1918, GBL, F. 358, 324/24.

26. N. A. Rubakin, "N. Lenin-Uljanow," *Internationale Rundschau,* no. 5 (March 15, 1918), pp. 97-105.

27. GBL, F. 358, 159/1-5. See also his series "Groote figuren der Russische Revolutie," *De Telegraaf* (Amsterdam), August 18, 19, 23, 24, September 2, October 18, November 8, and December 23, 1922, January 29, 1923.

28. See A. N. Rubakin, *Rubakin,* Rubakin, pp. 126-127.

29. GBL, *Zapiski otdela rukopisei,* 25: 437-438.

30. Ivanova et al., "Arkhiv N. A. Rubakina," GBL, *Zapiski otdela rukopisei,* 26: 113.

31. Undated letter, l, F. 358, 215/4.

32. Letter of September 10, 1917, GBL, F. 358, 215/4.

33. See his *Russian Sociology* (New York, 1915).

34. Correspondence in GBL, F. 358, 323/2.

35. Tikhomirov's letter of December 21, 1911, GBL, F. 358, 235/10.

36. Undated letter, presumably written in October 1917, GBL, F. 358, 323/2.

37. Letter of November 24, 1917, GBL, F. 358, 323/2.

38. Letter of November 24, 1917, GBL, F. 358, 197/32.

39. Letter of November 29, 1917, GBL, F. 358, 323/2.

40. Letter of December 2, 1917, GBL, F. 358, 323/2.

41. Hecker's letter to Rubakin, January 22, 1918, GBL, F. 358, 323/2.

42. Rolland, *Journal,* pp. 1373, 1412-1413.

43. Correspondence in GBL, F. 358, 323/2, 197/32.

44. Letter of June 11, 1918, GBL, F. 358, 323/2.

45. See Hecker's later publications: *Religion under the Soviets* (New York, 1927); *Religion and Communism* (New York, 1934); *Moscow Dialogues* (New York, 1934); *The Communist Answer to the World's Needs* (New York, 1934).

46. Public statement by the YMCA, GBL, F. 358, 323/2.

47. Letter of July 10, 1918, GBL, F. 358, 197/32.

VI: RUBAKIN AND SOVIET RUSSIA

1. Rolland, *Journal,* p. 1413.

2. See Alfred Erich Senn, *Diplomacy and Revolution: The Soviet Mission to Switzerland, 1918* (Notre Dame, 1974).

3. See Senn, "P. I. Biriukov," *The Russian Review,* 32: 283-285.

4. On the Swiss general strike, see Willi Gautschi, *Der Landes-streik 1918* (Zurich, 1968).

5. See Rolland, *Journal,* pp. 1658-1659.

6. A. N. Rubakin, *Rubakin,* p. 115.

7. Cf. Aref'eva, "N. A. Rubakin," *Kniga,* 8: 389.

8. See Biriukov's letters in 1919, GBL, F. 358, 208/17.

9 Correspondence published in GBL, *Zapiski otdela rukopisei,* 25: 424-429.

10. Karpinsky's letter published in ibid., 26: 399-404.

11. A. N. Rubakin, *Rubakin,* p. 119.

12. See Ivanova et al., "Arkhiv N. A. Rubakina," GBL, *Zapiski otdela rukopisei,* 26: 78-79.

13. E. Vinogradova, "K izucheniiu chitatelia," *Krasnyi bibliotekar',* 1925, no. 4, pp. 9-13.

14. *Sobranie zakonov,* ii, no. 42, art. 226, June 16, 1930. Rubakin received 250 rubles per month.

15. A. N. Rubakin, *Rubakin*, p. 125. On Rubakin's relations with Soviet intellectuals, see also Mavricheva, *N. A. Rubakin*, pp. 45-46; Ivanova et al., "Arkhiv N. A. Rubakina," GBL, *Zapiski otdela rukopisei,* '26: 107-112.

16. A. Rubinshtein, "V plenu u burzhuaznykh teoretikov. Antileninskie teorii v knigovedenii," *Zhurnalist,* 1932, no. 2, pp. 9-12.

18. See S. Simsova, ed., *Nicholas Rubakin and Bibliopsychology* (London, 1968), especially pp. 9-53.

19. See Rubakin's son's account of his efforts to trace the fate of the archive in A. N. Rubakin, *Rubakin,* pp. 163-166.

EPILOGUE

1. Burtsev to Rubakin, June 4, 1915, GBL, F. 358, 211/47.

2. N. A. Rubakin, *Sredi knig,* 3: 100-189. See also Senn, "The publication of *Sredi knig,*" ibid., 1: XXIII.

BIBLIOGRAPHY

A complete bibliography on Nicholas Rubakin's life and works could take up a book by itself. The bibliography of just his works, published in vol. 26 of the Lenin Library's *Zapiski otdela rukopisei,* extends to 55 pages and lists 766 items, including reprintings and published letters. When one considers also his archive, which runs to 313,179 pages contained in 492 boxes, then it becomes obvious that the bibliography offered below is a highly selective one.

Rubakin's enormous archive provides the basis for any study of his life and work. It includes his own manuscripts, some manuscripts written by others, letters from others which total over 75,000 pages, and a considerably smaller collection of his own letters. The other archival collections mentioned in section I contain either useful documentation relating to the milieu in which Rubakin worked or else include correspondence with him.

Of the studies listed, the most useful are those by his son A. N. Rubakin and by K. G. Mavricheva. A. N. Rubakin's biography of his father, a volume in the series "The Life of Remarkable People," is a highly personal document, useful more for its anecdotes than for its analysis. Mavricheva's study has concentrated more on Rubakin's bibliographical and on his writings, and it is more scholarly in tone and in presentation.

I: UNPUBLISHED SOURCES

Auswärtiges Amt, Bonn. Records of the German mission in Switzerland. Available also on microfilm, although filmed only selectively.

Bisk, Isaac, Papers. Nicolaevsky collection, Hoover Institution, Stanford, California.

League of Swiss Relief Societies for Political Prisoners and Exiles of Russia, International Institute of Social History, Amsterdam.

Lochner, Louis P., "Henry Ford and His Peace Venture," MS in

Louis P. Lochner Papers, Box 53, Wisconsin State Historical Society, Madison, Wisconsin.
Okhrana archive, Hoover Institution, Stanford, California.
Rubakin, N. A., Archive. Lenin Library, Moscow (GBL), Fond 358.

II: SELECTED PUBLICATIONS OF RUBAKIN

Correspondence with Maxim Gorky, GBL, *Zapiski otdela rukopisei*, 25: 424-429.
—with V. A. Karpinsky, ibid., 26: 399-404.
—with Romain Rolland, obid., 25: 432-463.
Etiudy o russkoi chitaiushchei publike. St. Petersburg, 1895.
"Groote figuren der Russische Revolutie," *De Telegraaf* (Amsterdam), August 18, 19, 23, 24, September 2, October 18, November 8, and December 23, 1922, January 19, 1923.
Introduction la psychologie bibliogique, 2 vols. Paris, 1922.
Opyt programmy issledovaniia literatury dlia naroda. St. Petersburg, 1889.
"Osnovnye zadachi bibliotechnogo dela," *Russkaia shkola,* 1907, no. 7-8, pp. 174-203.
Pered rassvetom. St. Petersburg, 1912.
Pis'ma k chitateliam o samoobrazovanii. St. Petersburg, 1913.
Praktika samoobrazovaniia. Moscow, 1914.
Rossiia v tsifrakh. 2d ed. Moscow, 1912.
Sredi knig. 2d ed. 3 vols. Moscow, 1911-1915, reprinted Cambridge, 1973.

III. BIBLIOGRAPHIES

Fridman, V. E., et al., "Trudy N. A. Rubakina," GBL, *Zapiski otdela rukopisei,* 26: 151-206.
Mavricheva, K. G., *N. A. Rubakin.* Moscow, 1972. Pp. 161-176.

IV: SECONDARY WORKS

Agafonov, V. A. *Zagranichnaia okhranka.* Petrograd, 1918.
Aref'eva, E. P., "N. A. Rubakin—kak knigosobiratel' i ego

biblioteki v Sovetskom Soiuze," *Kniga: Issledovaniia i materialy*, 8: 277-400.

Biriukov, P. I., *L. N. Tolstoi. Biografiia.* 3 vols. Berlin, 1921.

Bonch-Bruevich, V. D., "Biblioteka i arkhiv RSDRP v Zheneve," *Krasnaia letopis'*, 1931, no. 3, pp. 106-134.

Briskman, M. A., "Retsenziia V. I. Lenina na trud N. A. Rubakina i ego metodologicheskoe znachenie," *Trudy* (Leningradskii gos. institut kul'tury im. N. K. Krupskoi), 1971, no. 22, pp. 242-255.

Burtsev, Vladimir. *V pogone za provokatorami.* Moscow, 1928.

Derunov, K. M., *Primernyi bibliotechnyi katalog.* St. Petersburg, 1908-1911.

Filipov, Iu. F., *Emigratsiia. St. Petersburg,* 1906.

Gor'kii, M., *Sobranie sochinenii.* 30 vols. Moscow, 1949-1953.

Ivanova, L. M., A. B. Sidorova, M. V. Charushnikova, "Arkhiv N. A. Rubakina," GBL, *Zapiski otdela rukopisei,* 26: 63-206.

Keep, J. H. L., "1917: The Tyranny of Paris over Petrograd," *Soviet Studies,* 20: 22-35.

Lenin, V. I., *Polnoe sobranie sochinenii.* 55 vols. Moscow, 1960-1964.

Mashkova, M. V., "G. V. Plekhanov i 'Sredi knig' N. A. Rubakina," *Sovetskaia bibliografiia,* 1963, no. 6 (82), pp. 83-101.

—, *Istoriia russkoi bibliografii nachala XX veka (do Oktiabria 1917 goda).* Moscow, 1969.

Mavricheva, K. G., *N. A. Rubakin.* Moscow, 1972.

Possony, Stefan., *Lenin: Compulsive Revolutionary.* Chicago, 1964.

Razgon, L. V., *Pod shifrom "Rb."* Moscow, 1966.

Rolland, Romain, *Journal des annees de guerre 1914-1919.* Paris, 1952.

Rubakin, A. N., *Nad rekoiu vremeni.* Moscow, 1966.

—, *Rubakin (Lotsman knizhnogo moria).* Moscow, 1967.

Rubinshtein, A., "V plenu u burzhuaznykh teoretikov. Antileninskie teorii v knigovedenii," *Zhurnalist,* 1932, no. 2, pp. 9-12.

Senn, Alfred Erich, "Nikolai Rubakin's Library for Revolutionaries," *Slavic Review,* 32: 554-559.

—, "The Publication of *Sredi knig,*" in N. A. Rubakin, *Sredi knig,* 3 vols. (Cambridge, England, 1973), 1: V-XXVIII.

—, *The Russian Revolution in Switzerland, 1914-1917.* Madison, Wis., 1971.

Simsova, S., ed. *Nicholas Rubakin and Bibliopsychology.* London, N.Y., 1968.

Sytin, I. D., *Zhizn' dlia knig.* Moscow, 1960.

Tolstoi, Lev, *Polnoe sobranie sochinenii.* 90 vols. Moscow, 1928-1958.

Vinogradova, E., "K izucheniiu chitatelia," *Krasnyi bibliotekar'*, 1925, no. 4, pp. 9-13.